BERL ☑ S0-AYS-209

MADEIRA

By the staff of Berlitz Guides

How to use our guide

- All the practical information, hints and tips that you will need before and during the trip start on page 101.

- For general background, see the sections Madeira and the Madeirans, p. 6, and A Brief History, p. 12.

- All the sights to see are listed between pages 20 and 67, with the suggestions on excursions from Madeira from pages 70 to 78. Our own choice of sights most highly recommended is pinpointed by the Berlitz traveller symbol.

- Entertainment, nightlife and all other leisure activities are described between pages 79 and 92, while information on restaurants and cuisine is to be found on pages 93 to 100.

- Finally, there is an index at the back of the book, pp. 126–128.

Found an error or an omission in this Berlitz Guide? Or a change or new feature we should know about? Our editor would be happy to hear from you, and a postcard would do. Be sure to include your name and address, since in appreciation for a useful suggestion, we'd like to send you a free travel guide. Write to: Berlitz Publishing Company Ltd., London Road, Wheatley, Oxford OX9 1YR, England.

Although we make every effort to ensure the accuracy of all the information in this book, changes occur incessantly. We cannot therefore take responsibility for facts, prices, addresses and circumstances in general that are constantly subject to alteration.

Text: Ken Bernstein
Photography: Daniel Vittet
We would like to thank the Portuguese National Tourist Office and Gerardine White-Pereira, Patricia Guest and Julian Balkin for their help in preparing and updating this guide. We are also grateful to TAP-Air Portugal.

Cartography: 🅕 Falk-Verlag, Hamburg.

Contents

Madeira and the Madeirans

Madeira is an accessible island in the Atlantic Ocean, as beautiful as a South Pacific daydream. You can suntan all the year round in what is probably one of the best climates in the world. You can enjoy honest food and distinguished wine, priceless seascapes and sensational gardens.

The island is a bit less than 600 miles south-west of Lisbon, but much closer to the

coast of Africa. Every so often a hot wind called the *leste* blows in as a reminder.

Strictly speaking, Madeira is the name applied to a far-flung archipelago fanning out from the main island. Only one of the other isles is inhabited—the beach holiday hideaway of Porto Santo. Christopher Columbus lived there for a time; he married the governor's daughter. Today, as in the 15th century, all of the archipelago is con-

Vantage points on Madeira: afoot midst wild flowers above Funchal; bundled up in brother's basket.

sidered part of Portugal. The graceful red crosses painted on the sails of the caravels of Portugal's Prince Henry the Navigator can now be seen decorating the banners at every village celebration on Madeira.

The island's dimensions are small—only 35 miles long and 13 miles wide. But the terrain, contorted in the volcanic holocaust which created the island millions of years ago, is so mountainous and difficult that distances are magnified in practice. Some villagers have never ventured as far as the capital, Funchal. Though the island's area is only 286 square miles, its population is over 270,000. So many people in so small an area has caused massive emigration over the years. The most successful emigrants eventually return from Venezuela, South Africa or Brazil to build luxurious villas on Madeira, inspiring ambitious young islanders to try the same gamble.

After centuries of emigration and return, plus the presence of pirates, travel-

ling salesmen and occupying troops, the faces of Madeirans may remind you of faraway places. Some are as dark as a North African windburn, while the blue-eyed, blond-haired Madeirans may recall the 19th-century British garrisons. Whatever the family tree, they all share the language and culture of Portugal.

Nearly a third of the population congregates in Funchal, the island's political and economic capital and only real city. Built on hillsides overlooking a wide and spectacular south-coast bay, Funchal is where the cruise-ship passengers step ashore for a flurry of shopping and sightseeing. Less transient tourists are pampered in distinguished hotels along the western seafront of the city. The 20th-century wave of tourism expanded the hotel zone much further to the west and inspired other proposals for hotels and villas elsewhere around Madeira.

Wherever hotels haven't yet been built, Madeira's traditional agriculture remains the dominant influence. Depending on the altitude, the rich volcanic soil of the terraces produces tons of bananas and grapes

On the rocks: Madeira fishermen deal cards and wait for tide.

9

for the wine that has made the island famous. With all the sunshine a plant could want, plus abundant water supplies assured by an ingenious irrigation network, everything grows uncommonly well. In fact, nature's only unkindness has been towards the beaches. With one or two exceptions (and more developments are on their way), the beaches of Madeira are essentially sandless, with shingle and stone. Hotels, clubs and municipalities have compensated with plenty of swimming pools as well as facilities for getting in and out of the sea for a swim. Beach enthusiasts have to hop over to the island of Porto Santo for the real thing.

However, the seas around Madeira are fine for swimming, snorkelling, scuba diving, sailing, water skiing, and fishing—both serious and relaxed. (See the professional anglers come home with their prize catches of several breeds, especially a tasty deep-water monster called *espada*, or scabbard-fish.) Ashore, the sports possibilities include golf, tennis and even mountain climbing: Pico Ruivo, Madeira's summit, is more than 6,000 feet

high. Less energetic nature-lovers won't want to miss strolling among wild flowers along the *levadas*, or watercourses, arduously engineered over the centuries. Jaded city dwellers may be tempted to stay close to the luxury hotels with their night-clubs and gourmet restaurants; for exercise they can amble over to Funchal's casino for roulette, blackjack or chemin-de-fer until deep into the night.

For conventional sightseeing, a week's worth of organized coach tours covers most of the island's highlights, while boat trips give an addi-tional perspective to the sights. And if you don't mind tough driving on narrow mountain roads, hire a car and see for yourself. Wander into fishing villages and in-land market towns where children in woollen caps smile and wave to foreigners. See the farmers tilling tiny terraces the way their grandfathers did. Sniff a wild flower. Feed a lizard. Watch a butterfly. These are the pressing concerns on Madeira, hundreds of miles from the nearest worry.

Nature provided a sandy beach on nearby island of Porto Santo.

A Brief History

Madeira is the sort of place great men go to—before or after their prime. The echoes of momentous events have been heard here for almost six centuries, but the island is too relaxed, hidden too far beyond the mainstream of history, to make the headlines. Instead it trembles with the aftershocks, producing intriguing postscripts to history.

Footnote: Madeira put Henry the Navigator on the map. A man of ideas who rarely went to sea himself, Portugal's Prince Henry commissioned the expeditions which discovered and colonized Madeira. He proved that ships could sail beyond the sight of land, navigating scientifically regardless of prevailing winds, and come back safely. The discovery of Madeira in 1419 showed that treasure, not calamity, waited beyond the horizon. Prince Henry's students set the stage for Portugal's Golden Age, which culminated in undeniable confirmation that the world is round—Magellan's circumnavigation of the globe (1519–22).

Zarco Steps Ashore

The discovery of the Madeiran archipelago is credited to João Gonçalves Zarco, who sailed in the service of Prince Henry. In 1418 Zarco set foot on Porto Santo island. The next year his second expedition pushed further into the unknown and landed on a much larger, uninhabited island thick with forest, which he named Ilha da Madeira—"island of timber". The Portuguese Crown, elated at the news of a fertile new possession, immediately undertook a programme of colonization, and Zarco and his fellow navigator, Tristão Vaz Teixeira, became co-governors of Madeira.

While Zarco is officially glorified as an heroic explorer and statesman (he governed Funchal for more than 40 years), detractors consider him only one among a long line of possible discoverers of Madeira. Indeed, who can say that the Phoenicians didn't first set eyes on Madeira thousands of years ago? Another romantic school of thought suggests that the intrepid Irish voyager, St. Brendan, may have visited the island in the 6th century.

Footnote: a complicated legend tells of a shipwreck on

Sponsor of discovery of Madeira: Navigator Henry with moustache.

Madeira in the 14th century. It all begins with the elopement of an English pair named Robert Machim (or Machin, or perhaps even MacKean) and a certain Anne d'Arfet. To escape from the lady's tyrannical father, they had chartered a boat to France, but a terrible tempest eventually tossed them onto Madeira. According to the legend, the couple died soon after—she of exposure suffered during the storm, he of heartbreak. But enterprising crewmen cut down some of the trees at hand, built a raft and escaped to tell the story. When news of an Atlantic island reached Portugal, it provided the incentive for the Zarco expedition. Or so goes the tale, which also alleges that the Madeiran town of Machico was named in memory of the gallant Englishman.

Starting from Scratch

Whatever the legends and traditions, it's a fact that João Gonçalves Zarco found an uninhabited Madeira: no natives still living in stone-age conditions (as the Spaniards found on the Canary Islands), no ancient monuments or archaeological puzzles (like on Minorca). Civilization began on Madeira in the year 1419. Zarco's colonists had only what they brought along—plus unlimited fresh water rushing down the mountains and more timber than they knew what to do with.

To clear the land for agriculture, the settlers set fire

to Madeira's dense forest. According to one account, the island burned uncontrollably for five years. (Another version says seven years.) These stories may tax credulity but there certainly was an important, long-lasting fire; all eyewitness chronicles agree.

Within a few years, the land-reclamation programme paid off with Madeira's first crop: sugar-cane. Imported from Italy, it grew profusely in the semi-tropical sunshine, fertilized by the ashes left from the holocaust. Throughout Europe at this time, sugar was a luxury commanding very high prices, and thus Madeira took on sudden significance for the Portuguese economy. Not long after the sugar boom began, vines—brought to the island from Crete—began to produce sweet grapes from which creditable wines were made. The taste was distinctive, thanks to the combination of climate, volcanic soil and the layer of ash from the big blaze. The first Madeira wine to attract the attention of connoisseurs abroad was Malvasia, or Malmsey.

Footnote: about 15 years before he discovered America, Columbus sailed to Madeira on a routine merchant-shipping assignment. About this time, he met the daughter of Governor Bartolomeu Perestrelo of Porto Santo island. They married, settled for a while on Porto Santo and had a son. The Portuguese like to say that Columbus learned most of his seafaring skill from Portuguese sailors. What they don't like to recall is that Lisbon rejected his visionary plan to sail west to the Indies. So he took his theory instead to the Spanish monarchs, Ferdinand and Isabella.

Pirates Ahoy!
The 16th and 17th centuries were tempestuous. In 1566 a French pirate named Bertrand de Montluc arrived in Funchal harbour. It's unclear whether he arrived by chance, washed ashore during a storm, or was simply lured to Madeira by rumours of its multiplying riches. His three-ship armada invaded the island, unleashing an unforgettable 16 days of pillage and plunder.

In Europe, an invasion of greater global significance soon followed. In 1580, Spain's King Philip II proclaimed himself monarch of

Portugal and marched his army across the border to back up his pretensions. The Spanish occupation of Portugal, which included Madeira, lasted for 60 years. A highly visible relic of that era is the Forte do Pico ("Peak Fort"), up on the hillside overlooking Funchal harbour, now a communications station. As for relations between the Iberian neighbours, Spain didn't recognize the independence of Portugal until 1668.

Statue in Funchal centre honours the Portuguese discoverer, Zarco.

Funchal harbour from the sea, as pictured by a 17th-century artist.

England Enters the Scene

Madeira's traditional links with England began as early as the 17th century, when Charles II married Portugal's Catherine of Bragança in 1662: one provision of the formal wedding agreement granted special favours to English settlers on Madeira. This privilege was further enhanced by regulations covering British trade with the American colonies. Madeira wine became the only one which could be exported directly to the British zones of the Western hemisphere; all other had to be shipped via an English harbour aboard an English ship. The heady commercial possibilities attracted more Britons to Madeira. The community they founded constituted (until comparatively recently) the island's élite.

The British presence grew suddenly in 1801. British troops moved in to protect the island against a possible threat from France. They pulled out six months later, having kept the peace and made friends with the Madeirans. In 1807 the island seemed more vulnerable, for Napoleon had invaded the Portuguese mainland. The British sailed back and stayed until 1814 in the ambivalent roles of ally, protector and occupying power. Some reports say relations between the 4,000-man garrison and the islanders were less cordial this time.

Footnote: Napoleon abdicated for the second and last time on June 22, 1815. Two months later, on his way to exile and death on the British island of St. Helena in the South Atlantic, the deposed emperor caught a glimpse of romantic Madeira. His ship anchored off Funchal to take on supplies. The only visitor allowed aboard was the British consul, who presented Napoleon with some Madeira wine.

War and Pestilence

The second half of the 19th century was memorable for natural disasters. Cholera caused thousands of deaths in 1856. The vines were wiped out by blight in 1852—and again by insects in 1873. The sugar plantations suffered a plague in 1882.

More bad news: Portugal, which by now had collected a sizeable colonial empire in Africa, was forced into the First World War in 1916 when Germany declared war on the country after the seizure of some German ships in Lisbon harbour. Madeira's strategic significance for Atlantic shipping did not escape the Germans. In December 1916 a German submarine surprised three Allied ships in Funchal harbour, causing heavy losses. The U-boat escaped. Local lore says it was the same one that surfaced a year later and shelled the wireless station on the main sea-wall. Witnesses recall that a few shells overshot the target and exploded in the town, causing excitement but no casualties.

Portugal's sacrifices in the First World War led to a political and economic crisis which brought down the 17

Accelerating Pace

Since Victorian times the tourist business has been very important to Madeira. Wealthy sun-lovers, mostly English, could escape from winter here; cruise ships stopped at length; and suspected sufferers from consumption and other pulmonary complaints settled into villas, hotels and hospitals on the island's salubrious mountainsides.

Change came slowly. In 1921 a seaplane achieved the first flight from Lisbon to Funchal (commemorated by a small monument near the waterfront). A commercial seaplane service linking England, Lisbon and Madeira began in 1949, but a crash nine years later put an unexpected end to the experiment.

In 1960 the airport on Porto Santo opened; tourists had to transfer to a ship for the last leg of the journey to Madeira. Just four years later Madeira's own airport went into service, thereby ushering in an era of active tourist promotion which, even today, goes from strength to strength.

short-lived (1910–32) republican form of government.

Stability was achieved only at the cost of extreme authoritarian conservatism. Dr. António de Oliveira Salazar, who became minister of finance in 1928 and premier four years later, imposed a firm rule on the country. However, Salazar managed to keep Portugal out of the Second World War. When he retired after a massive stroke in 1968, the stern

The same age-old techniques ensure the same timeless quality: try a taste of all varieties of Madeira at an armazém.

reins were taken by a law professor, Dr. Marcello Caetano. The army overthrew the dictatorship in 1974, abandoning the debilitating colonial wars and introducing a novelty in modern Iberian history—free elections.

Footnote: when the army unseated President Américo Tomás and Prime Minister Caetano, the deposed leaders stopped at Madeira on their way to exile in Brazil. Unlike Napoleon, they were allowed ashore. But it was no holiday, for they were incarcerated in the 16th-century São Lourenço fortress overlooking the harbour and the broad Atlantic horizon.

Where to Go

On most maps Madeira rates no more than a dot. The island is unarguably small and far from civilization, but it should never be confused with one of those rockpiles jutting from the sea. Madeira is green, beautiful and big enough to get lost in.

With a couple of weeks to spare, you could see the highlights. Get to know the capital, Funchal, and then turn to the "provinces". Look down onto banana plantations, with orange-tiled roofs peeking through a jungle of trees, plants, vines and flowers. Welcome home the fishermen as they return from the deep, shyly showing off the big ones that didn't get away. Drink from a mountain spring. And if the sightseeing's too much, hide out for a couple of days on Porto Santo, the uncomplicated island with a perfect beach.

Lacking sandy beach, Porto Moniz exploits its natural ocean pools.

Funchal
Pop. 100,000

Cruise-ship passengers arriving in Funchal **harbour** see the entire panorama: squat white houses amidst tropical greenery, climbing the hills around a spacious bay. You can nearly match this view by strolling to the far end of Funchal's municipal *cais* (quay), which sticks straight out into the harbour from the centre of the town. From the jetty the scene can change while you watch. Clumps of innocent white clouds suddenly invade the heavenly blue sky; then foggy rainclouds slither down

the hillsides behind the town. But just as suddenly, a beam of sunlight strikes a white steeple, heralding a blazing sunset. After dark, Funchal twinkles as magically as the matching stars above it.

The *cais*, with its yacht marina, is where you get your bearings. Look out over the sweep of the harbour. The western part is enclosed by a man-made breakwater called the **Pontinha**, begun in the 18th century. It didn't reach its present size, less than a mile in length, until 1962. Watch the tugs straining to ease a cruise ship into its berth at the far end of the Pontinha. You can walk or drive round the harbour and out along the breakwater; stop to roam the old fortress (*Nossa Senhora da Conceição*) on the first of the islets used as a stepping stone for the jetty.

But now face inland from the *cais*. The **Avenida das Comunidades Madeirenses**, parallel to the waterfront, carries a noisy load of buses, cars and motorcycles. Here you can hire a taxi or join coach tours which show you the capital and the surroundings. But for the real feel of Funchal, an easy stroll is the best introduction.

A Walk Round Funchal

The far side of the Avenida das Comunidades Madeirenses is dominated by the

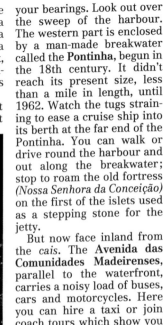

As fireworks signal a new year, Funchal merrymakers whoop it up. 23

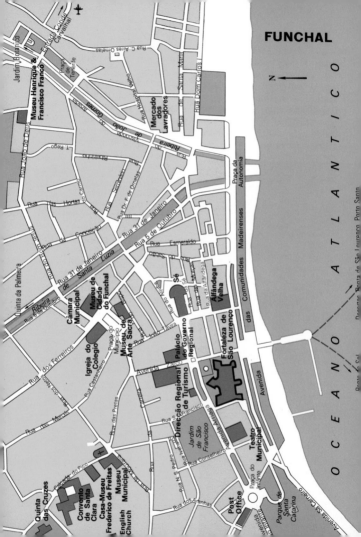

Fortaleza de São Lourenço (St. Lawrence Fortress). The 16th-century fort, a Portuguese national monument, contains the residence of Madeira's military governors. Historic cannons loom from notches in the walls, and white-gloved sentries with modern submachine guns guard the main gate. The fortress is closed to the public.

Walk up Avenida Zarco alongside the fortress. At the first main intersection (Avenida Arriaga) stands the statue of the island's discoverer, João Gonçalves Zarco. On the north-east corner is the **Palácio do Governo Regional**, the island's administrative headquarters. Notice the novel dimensions of the windows, protected by green shutters, and the ironwork of the gates. This impressive building surrounds a couple of admirable old patios.

From Avenida Arriaga, continue uphill to the top of Avenida Zarco and turn right. From here, you can see the **Praça do Município** (Municipal Square). The buildings on this square don't match each other but they're strikingly handsome.

The **Igreja do Colégio** (Collegiate Church) was founded in the 17th century. The façade contains so many harmonious yet unexpected elements that it's worth standing back and pondering: marble statues in niches and doors where windows ought to be. The adjoining college, run by the Jesuits until 1760 (when the order was banished from Portugal and its possessions), served as a barracks for British troops during the two occupations in the early 19th century.

The principal government building on this square, the **Câmara Municipal** (Town Hall), occupies an 18th-century palace. It houses the **Museu da Cidade do Funchal** (City Museum), tracing the capital's growth from the 15th century. The museum (open Monday to Friday from 9 a.m. to 12.30 p.m. and 2 to 5.30 p.m.) also shows watercolours of 19th-century Funchal scenes by English artists.

Behind the Town Hall, beyond its parking lot, is the Ribeira de Santa Luzia, one of Funchal's ravines. These rugged riverbeds carry excess rainwater from the mountains to the sea. Here, in the centre of town, the ravines are discreetly covered with trellises of bou- 25

gainvillea, concealing the litter accumulated below. If you hear only a trickle, don't be lulled into thinking the *ribeira's* great walls no longer serve a purpose; at certain times of the year the rush of water can barely be contained.

The building housing the **Museu de Arte Sacra** (Sacred Art Museum) faces the Praça do Município, but the entrance is at Rua do Bispo 21. The museum (open 10 a.m. to 12.30 p.m. and 2 to 5.30 p.m. from Tuesday to Saturday; on Sundays from 10 a.m. to 1 p.m.; closed Mondays) contains the best of the religious paintings, sculpture and vestments from all the island's old churches. Quite a few of the paintings are 15th- and 16th-century Flemish works which reached Madeira in the course of the early prosperous years of the sugar trade with Flanders.

A little further down Rua João Tavira, Madeira's **Sé** (Cathedral) comes into view. Big enough to be imposing by local standards, it's small enough to be crowded even for minor holy days. Local volcanic stone shows in the construction, with parts of the walls whitewashed to contrast with the natural colour. A tiled, pointed roof tops the square belfry. The simple architecture of the stone-and-whitewash façade conveys a feeling of quiet dignity.

Inside the Sé, notice the graceful arches. This was the first of Portugal's overseas cathedrals, begun in the 15th century. In the general obscurity, it's difficult to perceive the finely worked Moorish **ceiling** of cedar and ivory which is intricately carved in Manueline style—named after King Manuel I, who ruled Portugal at the height of the age of exploration. The designs show the exotic discoveries of those days—strange animals, flowers and trees, and a world·that was round instead of flat. A venerated local version of Our Lady of Fátima (the real shrine is located north of Lisbon) is usually surrounded here by a small conflagration of votive candles.

The cathedral's principal portal faces Funchal's main east-west artery, **Avenida Arriaga**. In the spring, the jacaranda trees put forth their fragrant blossom, and the avenue becomes a riot of colour. The birds in the trees look as if they've just popped over from the highlands of Africa. At dusk they chirp in syncopation.

At Avenida Arriaga 16–18, you'll find the **Direcção Regional de Turismo**, the official tourist office. Maps and literature are available here, and the multilingual receptionists know the answers to every imaginable question about the island and its facilities.

Several companies producing Madeira wines jointly operate what is called an **adêga** ("old wine lodge") to be found in the buildings just next to the tourist office. Visitors are invited to look at memorabilia of distinguished clients while tasting all four varieties of Madeira wines. You can buy bottles to take home, but don't feel

obliged; you can continue your tastings at other lodges and shops around the town before deciding which varieties and brands you prefer (see also pp. 97–98).

Just beyond this point is the **Jardim de São Francisco,** a municipal park and refuge of exquisite trees and flowers. Here you can have your shoes shined or just sit and wait for tiny lizards to venture into view. A family of black swans resides in the park's pond.

Across the avenue from the park is the Teatro Municipal, of classic design used as a theatre concert hall and cinema. Next door, the façade of a distinctive old building is tiled with illustrations of typical island

Sacred art at the Museu de Arte Sacra; Madeira's Sé at Christmas.

activities. A sign of the times: this most characteristic Madeiran building is now a salesroom for Japanese cars.

At the western end of Avenida Arriaga, next to Praça do Infante, lies one of Funchal's modern shopping centres with stores open seven days a week, restaurants, a bank and, across the square, an imposing post office.

More Sights: Uphill

A former aristocratic home, the **Museu Municipal** (Municipal Museum), at Rua da Mouraria 31, is now dedicated to natural history. In the modest aquarium on the ground floor you can watch the activities of beautiful, awesome specimens from local and distant seas. Upstairs, more of the same, but out of the water; models and mounted fish, birds and small animals of the island. (Open daily except Monday; afternoons only weekends.)

The **Convento de Santa Clara** (St. Clare's Convent), up the hill, was founded in the 15th century; rebuilt in the 17th century, it's now a

In patio of Funchal's main market fresh fruit fills wicker trays; nearby, fishermen talking shop.

school run by Franciscan nuns. There are orange trees in the curious old cloister. The inside walls of the adjoining church are fully tiled, giving it the appearance of a mosque. Pictures and designs fill the ceiling—the height of Manueline extravagance. In a niche in the rear wall of the church is the tomb of Madeira's discoverer, Zarco, who is said to have also founded this house of worship.

During his successful career as governor, Zarco is thought to have lived further up the hill, in the **Quinta das Cruzes** (Estate of the Crosses). The main house is now a museum of antiques, porcelain, artefacts and paintings.

The house is surrounded by a large, well-tended park. In addition to many other exotic flowers and plants, there's a magnificent orchid section (best seen in March and April). And students of history will be fascinated by the "archaeological garden", an outdoor display of relics from the oldest places on the island—tombstones, chunks of official buildings, a church window and the 15th-century pillory of the city of Funchal. (The museum is open from 10 a.m. to 12.30 p.m. and 2 to 6 p.m., Tuesday to Saturday, from 10 a.m. to 1 p.m. on Sundays; closed on Mondays.)

The road separating Quinta das Cruzes from the Convento de Santa Clara leads to a lookout point with a good **view** over the town and port. You'll see a grandiose dome in a park below. This is the English Church, an elaborate edifice testifying to the size and importance of the British colony as early as the beginning of the 19th century.

On the Waterfront

The beautifully restored **Alfândega Velha** (Old Customs House), a 16th-century Manueline monument, began a new career as part of the local parliament. (The deputies actually hold forth in the modernistic round building on the sea avenue.) Notice the regal doorways and oddly placed windows.

Make your way down Rua da Alfândega across the Ribeira de Santa Luzia and Ribeira de João Gomes to get to Funchal's main market. Built in 1941, it is called **Mercado dos Lavradores** (Workers' Market) because it faces a square called Praça dos Lavradores. The local colour couldn't be more concentrated and authentic: the women in native costumes selling flowers; fruit-vendors with their produce piled upon shallow wicker baskets lined with cabbage leaves; the fish department, where experts fillet the local speciality, *espada*—a vicious-looking black giant, long and thin in fighting trim. The Mercado dos Lavradores is the epitome of an Atlantic island market, built around a delightful patio which is ablaze with flowers. Buy an apple or a plastic bag of *tremoços* (lupin seeds), the small yellow beans which Madeirans eat like sunflower seeds, spitting out the skin.

Further east along the waterfront is Funchal's most colourful district, the **fishermen's quarter.** The narrow cobbled streets, the stronghold of artisans, have more than their quota of boisterous bars and seafood restaurants. Along the seafront here you'll find a small park and restaurant; a dry dock; the 17th-century Fortaleza de Santiago (St. James's

Sturdy Fortaleza de Santiago houses Madeira's coast guards.

Fort), an army barracks, closed to the public; and the **Igreja de Santa Maria Maior** (Church of St. Mary Major), a fine 18th-century church with elegant lines. On May 1 each year, a ceremony here commemorates Funchal's rescue from two great plagues of the 16th century; the miracles are attributed to the Apostle St. James the Less.

Glorious Gardens

A short bus ride (No. 30 from the Sea Avenue) into the hills northeast of Funchal takes you to the **Jardim Botânico** (Botanical Garden), the island's most comprehensive public garden. If you're driving yourself, try not to get lost. This splendid park is situated at the end of a new, wide road called Rua Carlos Azevedo de Menezes, named after a local botanist.

All the plants, flowers and trees which grow on Madeira are here, carefully labelled in Portuguese and Latin to settle arguments. The terraces luxuriate in tropical flowers; others are produced in greenhouses. The bonus

The island's flora in one garden: Jardim Botânico, above Funchal.

here is a grand view over the harbour.

Alongside the botanical garden, the **Jardim dos Loiros** (Tropical Bird Garden) is home to hundreds of exotic parrots—cockatoos and lorikeets, parakeets and macaws. They come in all colour combinations, some outra-

generations, it has shrubs and trees from all the world, including a lush array of subtropical plants. Between October and April thousands of camellias flower here, from white to pink and red.

Although the house is not open to the public, the

geous. Both the botanical and parrot gardens charge admission; both are open daily including Sundays and public holidays.

The 30-acre private garden of the **Quinta do Palheiro**, on the road to Camacha, belongs to Adam and Christina Blandy. Established over several

garden can be visited on weekday mornings. Tickets and garden brochures are on sale at the main gate. Many holiday companies include coach excursions here, and visitors can wander contentedly through the garden surrounded by the incessant croaking of frogs.

Outskirts of Funchal

Monte (which means simply "mount") is a hill-town above Funchal, full of fresh air and nostalgia. The good atmosphere brought sick European aristocrats to Monte in the 19th century. Their villas and the rest-homes for pulmonary patients contribute to melancholy overtones. During the Second World War, with tourism virtually non-existent, the Victorian funicular railway connecting Funchal and Monte was abandoned. Nowadays, buses and cars have easier ways of mounting to Monte; but for the descent, there are the famous snowless toboggans, called *carros de cesto*. It's at your risk, obviously, and not for the faint-hearted. Accidents have been known to occur, but many tourists find the experience exhilarating, as is confirmed by the volume of squeals...

Carros de cesto are really upholstered wicker chairs

Catching a breath on the way up to Our Lady of the Mount Church.

mounted on runners. The drivers, wearing white uniforms, straw hats and thick rubber-soled boots, lean far backwards on the run, restraining the sledge by a rope.

At the bottom of the run, the toboggan-handlers sometimes hop into a taxi to rush back to the summit for the next round of clients. The empty sledges follow on the back of a lorry.

Before you toboggan away from Monte, be sure to visit its richly decorated **Igreja de Nossa Senhora do Monte** (Our Lady of the Mount Church). Set in an evergreen park, it's dedicated to Madeira's patron saint. On Assumption Day, August 15, thousands of islanders make a pilgrimage to this church to kiss the holy image. Some climb the long flight of steps on their knees.

The church was constructed in the 18th century on the remains of a 15th-century chapel, said to have been built by the first Madeirans born on the island (twins named Adam and Eva). In a chapel on the left is the tomb of the last of the Austro-Hungarian emperors, Charles I of Austria (Charles IV of Hungary). He came to live in

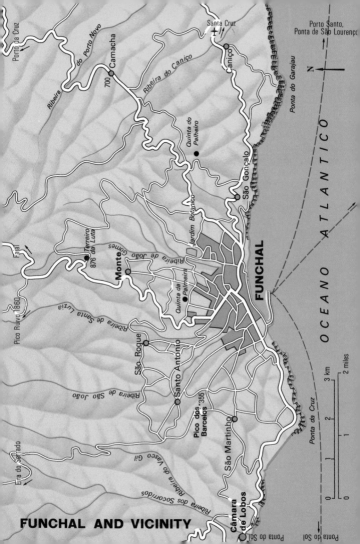

FUNCHAL AND VICINITY

Riding in Style

The slippery cobblestones of Funchal's streets, less than ideal for carefree strolling, make possible a distinctive method of transport.

Carros de cesto, toboggans powered by gravity, transport tourists from Monte down to Funchal (but not vice-versa). White-suited drivers run alongside the sleds manipulating steering ropes. Many find this type of locomotion exhilarating; others are less enthusiastic and put it on a par with the Ferris wheel for thrills one can live without.

Until a few years ago tourists could traverse difficult parts of the country majestically reclining in hammocks carried by skilled mountaineers. But better roads and growing objections to humans working as beasts of burden ended that era.

Progress, for better or worse, has taken its toll of Madeira's unique modes of transport.

Straw-hatted toboggan-pushers start tourists down from Monte.

Monte with his wife, the Empress Zita, after he abdicated in 1918. Charles died here in 1922, at the early age of 35, just as the hilltown's fashionable era was at its zenith.

Terreiro da Luta, at an altitude of 2,873 feet, provides a fine panorama of the town and harbour of Funchal. Terreiro da Luta is where the figure of Our Lady of the Mount, revered at the Monte church, was discovered under miraculous circumstances in the 15th century.

Fountain of Youth?

Time smiles on Madeira and its renowned dessert wines. They can live to be a hundred and still taste delicious. As a practical matter, you can keep a bottle of Madeira for years, corked or open, and drink it anytime with pleasure.

Madeira is still aged according to a complex old formula, and the traditional harvest is still seen in country areas. Common Market regulations regarding the export of Madeira require modern processes which curtail the festivity of the harvest somewhat. Instead of music, dancing and barefooted stamping on the grapes, there's likely

---

to be a businesslike weighing-in ceremony. Then a monstrous mincing machine crushes up to 100 pounds of grapes in one go. The juice used to be rushed to the producers' lodges in a 12-gallon goatskin carried on a man's back; with today's roads, it's normally put in casks and transported by lorry.

In the lodges the juice ferments. Then the new wine is slowly heated for three months in an *estufa*, or hothouse, at temperatures above 100° F. This simulates the effects of a long sea voyage across the equator and back, which is how Madeira wines were in fact improved—accidentally.

Madeira wines come in four varieties, from the dry Sercial to sweet Malmsey. In 1478 the Duke of Clarence was reported to have drowned himself in a butt of Malmsey wine. Better to stick to sipping Madeira before or after dinner. During a visit to the island you can become an expert in these sunny wines.

A rare sight... The traditional way to carry wine and other goods.

Now Madeira's biggest monument stands on the summit. It's dedicated to Our Lady of Peace in gratitude for the end of the First World War (in which Funchal suffered isolation, hunger and shelling). Round the monument are anchor chains from the Allied ships sunk in the harbour by German torpedoes. A small chapel here rounds out the facilities of Terreiro da Luta.

Pico dos Barcelos, with a restful, flower-gardened lookout point, stands at 1,164 feet. The panoramic view provides an insight into the geographical situation of Funchal.

If you're driving unhurriedly back to town, you might like to track down the exceptionally graceful hill church, visible from Pico dos Barcelos and other vantage points. Back roads will take you to the modern church of São Martinho with its unusually slender bell tower. It turns out to be ten times the size you would expect—a lavishly decorated cathedral-sized parish church set down in the midst of farmland. Discovering São Martinho will help convince you that on Madeira there's a surprise round every corner.

Circumnavigation

Although the roads are much improved, the coastline of Madeira is long and sinuous, so you wouldn't want to try driving all round the island in a single day. To simplify the organization of this chapter, though, we've listed the coastal towns in geographical order, starting from Funchal and heading west in a clockwise circuit of the island.

Câmara de Lobos is a fishing port 9 kilometres west of Funchal. Grizzled fishermen, manning brightly painted boats, sort, clean and pack their catch indifferent to the stares of foreigners. Câmara de Lobos is all business, but you will find restaurants and bathing facilities.

From out at sea, or from any vantage point above the town, Câmara de Lobos couldn't be more romantic: seagulls nest on the sharp volcanic shoals enclosing the harbour; fishermen's houses

Tenacious farmers grow crops on rugged cliffside at Cabo Girão.

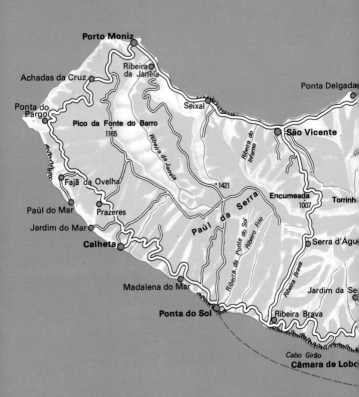

OCEANO

Porto Moniz

Ribeira
da Janela

Achadas da Cruz

Ponta Delgada

Ponta do
Pargo

Pico da Fonte do Barro
1165

Seixal

Ribeira do Inferno

São Vicente

Ribeira da Janela

· 1421

Encumeada
1007

Torrinh

Fajã da Ovelha

Paúl da Serra

Paúl do Mar

Prazeres

Serra d'Águ

Jardim do Mar

Calheta

Ribeira da Ponte do Sol

Ribeiro Frío

Madalena do Mar

Jardim da Se

Ribeira Brava

Ponta do Sol

Ribeira Brava

Cabo Girão

Câmara de Lobo

MADEIRA

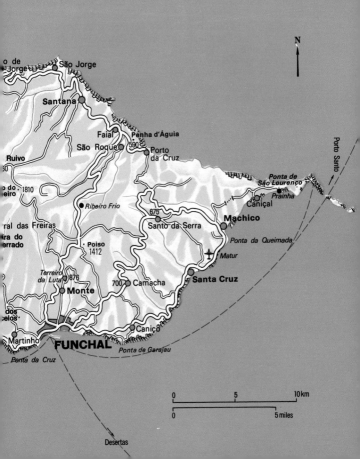

cling to the rocky hillsides and carefully terraced vineyards rise behind the beach. Sir Winston Churchill used to come here to paint this prototype of an island port.

Câmara de Lobos means "lair of the sea-wolves", a name bestowed by Madeira's earliest settlers when they discovered seals among the rocks. Nowadays fishermen still catch *espada*, or scabbard-fish, at one time the island's staple food. Notice the small white chapel on the waterfront, an early 15th-century project rebuilt in 1723.

Beyond Câmara de Lobos the road climbs for 10 kilometres through some of Madeira's richest agricultural country until it reaches the summit of a headland named **Cabo Girão**. No distraction—even if you're surrounded by a crowd of tourists—can spoil Cabo Girão's appeal to the spirit. From the railing the view is more than 1,900 feet straight down onto the Atlantic. Agapanthus cling to the top of the promontory; pine and eucalyptus grow to the very edge. But a greater tenacity than this can be seen: hundreds of feet below, farmers have salvaged tiny plots of arable land, terracing them out and giving them the appearance of green postage stamps glued to the bottom of the cliff. This evidence of human indomitability is as inspiring as the power of the Atlantic waves beating below.

RIBEIRA BRAVA, meaning

"wild ravine", is an important town because it's the junction between the south-coast highway and a major north-south road. Steep hills rise on two sides of the town. The sea is a barrier in front, behind are the mountains and in between is a wide, unspoilt beach, with traditional-style shopping centre and cafés across the road. A modest square shaded by plane trees is cobbled with egg-shaped black stones from the beach.

Abundant water greens island's hillsides, whitens family wash.

The old white church has a steeple tiled in a checkerboard pattern, blue and white. Colourful, too, are the outer walls of the local market. Like the school walls, they are decorated with scenes of Madeiran life painted by children. The local bars are unpretentious; a glass of the regional *aguardente* (firewater) costs less than a fizzy drink.

Considering the terrain, 48 the road along the south coast is more than adequate as far west as PONTA DO SOL, which is a district capital with a rocky beach and a fine old church. Beyond it, too, the old narrow, bumpy, difficult road has been greatly improved.

Less than 10 kilometres beyond Ponta do Sol you may welcome a break at a belvedere overlooking MADALENA DO MAR. Far below—again, straight down—is a completely unspoilt beach. Even

from the great height of the lookout point, you can hear the ocean polishing and re-arranging the stones.

CALHETA, the next significant town to the west, is a centre of banana plantations and vineyards. The parish church, rebuilt in 1639, is notable for a complex Moorish-style ceiling.

A tough slog of nearly 50 kilometres covers the western extremity of Madeira and ends on the north coast

Fishermen return regularly with big catches; Câmara de Lobos, Madeira's most colourful port.

at Porto Moniz. This area, until recent years a virtual wilderness, is now well populated, and there are some beautiful villas.

The village of PORTO MONIZ, right at the top of the island, is set high on a hill 49

over the seafront. The most interesting part is an afterthought of a peninsula, a volcanic extension into the Atlantic. The **reefs** here form natural pools, completed by chunks of concrete, put there to fill some crucial gaps. Here you can swim in running seawater, immune to the fury of the north coast's tides. These unusual pools have made Porto Moniz something of a tourist attraction. Big restaurants along the shore are geared to producing lunches for coachloads of day-trippers.

If it's been too warm for you on the south coast of Madeira you'll appreciate the fresh breezes at Porto Moniz. Just around the point from the tourist area is the town's fishing port.

A major event in town is the annual cattle fair, held every August.

Heading east from Porto Moniz on the north-coast

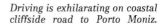

Driving is exhilarating on coastal cliffside road to Porto Moniz.

Inland here you can see one of Madeira's four hydro-electric power stations. Water rushing down from the mountains to the sea provides not only irrigation and drinking water but also abundant electrical power.

Soon after the town of SEIXAL, a wine-growing centre, the road passes a **waterfall** tumbling dramatically in a thin cascade from the top of a cliff. You can stop for a drink of fresh mountain water. (Another waterfall along this road will give your car a free wash, whether you need it or not.)

road is an adventure. In places the highway hugs the shore, just above the waves. Then it climbs the mountainside, clinging to a narrow foothold chipped out of the rock. Several tunnels, cutting through the cliffs, look as if they had been hollowed out with picks and shovels.

RIBEIRA DA JANELA (Ravine of the Window) is named after the window-like opening in a rock formation just offshore.

Between Seixal and São Vicente the coastal road crosses another ravine carrying rainwater to the sea. Glimpsing RIBEIRA DO INFERNO (Ravine of Hell) from the road, you get an impressive, though sinister, view of a rain forest. It leads up to Madeira's only stretch of moorland, a mysterious plateau in the centre of the island, called Paúl da Serra (see p. 63). **51**

High on a precipitous hilltop above SÃO VICENTE is a strange church—actually a clockless clock tower surmounting a small chapel dedicated to Our Lady of Fátima. Down in the village itself, the parish church is worth a visit. The interior is decorated with colourful tiles, elaborate scrollwork, frescoes and paintings. On the ceiling is a picture of the village including the church itself. With an abundance of flowers and trees, São Vicente is a beautiful town, and there are many facilities for visitors. The centre is sheltered inland from the harsh ocean winds. On the coast, a small chapel has been hollowed out of the rock. You can't miss it. It's at the spot where the picturesque coastal road meets the main north-south road. (The latter—it takes you as far as Ribeira Brava—would cut 90 kilometres from the round-the-island route we've theoretically taken between Funchal and São Vicente.)

The fertile peninsula of PONTA DELGADA juts bravely into the ocean. An attractive white church, a natural pool for safe sea bathing, and distinguished old houses provide the interest here.

Vineyards, protected from north winds by barriers of gorse, continue to SÃO JORGE. The village has a richly ornamented 17th-century church.

Then continue clockwise along the north coast on to the next important village, **Santana**—so full of charm that it's almost too good to be true. Some of the families of this village live in fairytale cottages with steeply pointed thatched roofs. This is essentially the same architectural style used elsewhere on Madeira for cattle shelters. But here the tourist authorities hold competitions for the prettiest old cottages, with prizes for colour schemes, hedges and gardens. In any event, the government forbids the destruction of any of these houses. Aside from Santana's cottages, the

Machico: Madeira's first town (left); the happy sound of music.

district is delightful because of the altitude (about 1,300 feet) and the rolling hills full of apple trees and wild flowers.

After Santana, the big 53

Macaws and Mandarins

Madeira was the first overseas possession to which the Portuguese language was transplanted. It soon spread to far continents, creating a long-lasting linguistic empire. Today, Portuguese is still the official tongue in places as distant and different as Brazil and Macao.

During the golden age of exploration, Portuguese navigators brought back the vocabulary of the mysterious East. It was these explorers who gave us such terms as macaw, mandarin, pagoda and verandah. They also named the dodo bird (after the Portuguese word for stupid).

white church of FAIAL dominates the seaside plain. Then, as the road climbs beyond Faial's vineyards and terraces, there are impressive views of the **Penha d'Águia** (Eagle Rock). This titanic rock formation, the north-coast equivalent of Cabo Girão on the south, sets the stage for the entire stretch of coastline. The last town before the road turns inland, PORTO DA CRUZ, is a tidy village with a bright, white modern church. From here you can see the easternmost peninsula, PONTA DE SÃO LOURENÇO.

On a map, the peninsula resembles the proboscis attached to a swordfish-shaped Madeira. In real life it's a desolate arm attached to a fertile body. The appendage ends with a rocky point separated from "mainland" Madeira by a 500-foot channel often writhing with heavy tides. On the rock is a lighthouse station, with its own miniature harbour.

The peninsula's skyline betrays almost no sign of civilization except for the towers of a communications station and a hilltop chapel dedicated to Our Lady of Piety. A long walk down the steep hillside from the chapel leads to Madeira's only sandy beach, PRAÍNHA. The sand is black. You can get to Praínha by boat—it's a one-and-a-half hour excursion from Funchal. Or if you'd rather drive, there's a very good road from Caniçal, Madeira's easternmost town.

CANIÇAL, an important fishing port, has grown out of recognition with the development of a free port zone along the coast here. Plans call for factories, warehouses and offices. Despite the boom-town atmosphere, Caniçal is a pretty village, with some of the best fish restaurants on the island. You can watch the fishermen going home from work, each carrying a wicker basket in one hand, some fish for lunch in the other.

Before the construction of Madeira's longest tunnel, on the road between Caniçal and Machico, the eastern corner of the island was completely isolated. There's no ready explanation for the large proportion of blond, blue-eyed children here.

MACHICO can claim to be Madeira's first town. This is where the Portuguese navigator João Gonçalves Zarco first came ashore in 1419. His fellow traveller and navigator, Captain Tristão Vaz Teixeira, ruled the eastern half of the island from Machico. There's a statue of him in front of Machico's 15th-century **parish church.** King Manuel I himself contributed a statue and distinguished portal to the church, an example of the exuberant style bearing his name. On top of the principal

Dramatic view from Ponta São Lourenço of Caniçal, Madeira's easternmost town.

chandelier a gilt angel blows his trumpet.

From Machico's triangular square several streets lead to the seafront. Until recent times, most of the shops in these streets displayed no signs or identification, since everyone knew what they sold anyway. Facing the beach, a triangular fort with an inscription dated 1706 provides a not-very-imposing defence establishment. The curve of Machico's harbour

is appealing, and the stony beach is fine for swimmers and sunbathers.

Just to the south of PONTA DA QUEIMADA, within walking distance of Machico, Madeira's largest tourist complex, a development called MATUR, consists of villas, flats and a major hotel adding up to accommodation for 4,000 holiday-makers. The facilities include bars, restaurants, swimming pools, tennis

courts, billiard tables, a
sauna and a supermarket.
There is a beach a short distance from Matur.

Between Matur and Santa
Cruz lies the island's airport.
From the elevation of the
Matur development or from
the highway beyond Santa
Cruz, there are dramatic
views of the airfield.

SANTA CRUZ is an agree-
able town with a shingle
beach and organized bathing
facilities. The 16th-century

Fishermen of Caniçal haul their
catch from the sea to the beach.
Left: cottage in pretty Santana.

parish church contains less
clutter than most; its wooden
ceiling is painted with
scrollwork designed to give
a three-dimensional effect.
Across the town square the
town hall, though modern-
ized, retains a pair of splendid Manueline windows.
The courthouse, a few streets 57

away, is a remarkable 16th-century structure with sweeping verandahs and an impressive main staircase. Along the seafront, the modern municipal market is adorned with a cheerful frieze portraying fishermen and farmers at work. For all its importance as a district centre, Santa Cruz manages to avoid most of the disadvantages of busy town life.

CANIÇO is noted for its onions. The village encircles a large, imposing-looking church, garlanded on holy days with a profusion of paper flowers. The road downhill from there leads to modern villas.

A tourist development, Dom Pedro, extends towards the tip of PONTA DO GARAJAU. This cape has been an unmistakable Madeiran landmark since 1927, when nearby residents sponsored the construction of a tall statue of Jesus with arms outstretched. It's reminiscent of the one overlooking the harbour of Rio de Janeiro, though much smaller.

The long, steep, cobbled road from Garajau leads up to the main highway and, after a couple of kilometres, to the metropolitan area of Funchal.

Invisible Cows

You could tour the Madeiran countryside for a week and not come across a cow. Yet the island has an important dairy industry which supplies much of the milk, butter and cheese consumed by local residents and tourists. The cows are there, but invisible. They're confined to quarters.

Madeira's terrain is so steep and rocky that potential pastures are liable to be hazardous to the health of grazing cattle. They could easily fall from a precipice or at least onto the next terrace.

If the cows can't forage for food, the feed can be delivered to the cows. These bovine counterparts of battery-fed chickens never leave their thatched huts except for cleaning and milking. Farmers say the huts keep the cows cool in summer, warm in winter, dry in the rain and generally cozy. Some farmers live in a similar type of hut.

For hard-working team of farmers, no time to enjoy the ocean view.

Highland Sights

The rugged mountain chain splitting Madeira into northern and southern halves compounds the complexity of the climate. At a given moment it may be sunny and warm in Funchal, windy and misty on the north coast and snowing at the centre of the island. The ocean cloud formations zero-in on the peaks, producing a bounteous water supply but sometimes spoiling the view.

Like highland communities everywhere, Madeira's hill villages are different. Here are a few of the places to see, listed in alphabetical order.

CAMACHA. At a refreshing altitude of nearly 2,300 feet, this village is in the heart of willow country. As a result, it's the hub of the island's important wicker industry. Perhaps 2,500 people in the region are involved, one way or another, in making items such as wicker chairs or wicker sculptures. Since most of these craftsmen work at home, you may not actually see nimble fingers braiding the bleached osier into baskets, handbags and trays. But you'll probably come across farmers hauling stupendous loads of willow on their backs and artisans carrying their finished products to the wholesale buyers.

Camacha villagers are proud of their flowers and folk dancing. They also claim that the local football field was the scene of the first soccer match ever played in Portugal. The sport went on to become as much of an addiction here as elsewhere in Europe.

Eira do Serrado. This 3,300-foot lookout point is a mere 14 kilometres by road from Funchal. But what a drive! The road climbs in steep, hair-pin bends from the level of the banana plantations to laurel and eucalyptus country and, ultimately, to an environment of pine trees and bracing air. From the lookout point, there's an inspiring **view** down into a deep valley surrounded by volcanic mountains, often mistaken for a volcanic crater. Amazingly, the valley contains fertile farmland and the neat tile-roofed houses of a village. This improbable outpost of civilization is called

Basket craft: wicker workers of Camacha at their cottage industry.

61

Curral das Freiras, which means "nuns' shelter". The name derives from the story of a 16th-century pirate raid on Funchal, when the nuns of the Santa Clara Convent fled to the hills and finally down into the valley. Protected from the eyes of invaders and the unkindness of mountain winds, the settlement eventually became permanent. Rich volcanic soil and sunshine combined to support the hidden village, famous for its cherries and the liqueur Ginja. For centuries the only way to reach Curral das Freiras was over a difficult mountain footpath. Then a road brought the conveniences—and perils—of the outside world.

Encumeada. At almost the same altitude as Eira do Serrado, the mountain pass of Encumeada is the crest of the north-south route linking São Vicente and Ribeira Brava. The road climbs from sea level through a long, narrow valley strung with telephone and electricity wires as well as lush semi-tropical greenery. Finally, at Encumeada, you get a **view** over

Seemingly hopeless hills over the seashore are tamed by terracing.

great expanses of mountain scenery, providing an insight into the tormented geological development from thousands of years ago. On a clear day, face north and you see the sea, do a 180-degree turn and the sea appears again. All in all, a fantastic sight, wherever you look.

PAÚL DA SERRA may sound like a man's name, but it's Portuguese for "marsh of the mountain range". This accurately describes Madeira's moorland, occupying a plateau nearly 4,700 feet above sea level. The marshy table-land of 6 square miles is desolate but for occasional flocks of sheep. Because it's remote and so different from the usual Madeiran scenery, Paúl da Serra attracts hikers. But mist and fog frequently settle in, so tourists are officially warned that it's essential to travel here with a guide.

Pico do Arieiro, at more than 5,900 feet, is Madeira's second-highest peak. Above the Poiso Pass the road becomes dangerous, but not because of hills and bends. The sheep which graze in this district are so unaccustomed to traffic that they may innocently wander into your path and leave only with a lot of persuasion. If cars are a novelty to the sheep, so are the sheep a novelty to the traveller. This is one of the few areas of the island where any farm animals are seen. As the road rises the rugged countryside becomes more fascinating —great, plunging volcanic hillsides, mercifully green with plant life softening the topographical violence.

You don't have to be a mountain-climber to reach the summit of Arieiro. The road, 23 kilometres from Funchal, goes right to the top, where a lookout point provides a 360-degree **panorama.** You survey stratified canyon walls, boulders flung across the scene of volcanic catastrophe and a field of frozen lava—altogether, a festival of geology. In summer the terrain is parched; in winter it's sometimes covered with snow. At any time of year your visibility might suddenly be reduced by the arrival of clouds. This is a good excuse to sit out the weather in Pico do Arieiro's pousada.

Pico Ruivo, the top of Madeira, is at an altitude of 6,105 feet. Although this isn't strikingly higher than Arieiro, the peak is consider- **63**

ably harder to reach. Ruivo isn't as difficult to climb as it might seem; all you need are time and energy enough to walk an hour or two in each direction. Artists, poets and other romantics say it's worth going to great lengths to watch the sunrise from atop Pico Ruivo (which means "red peak"). The only feasible way this can be done is to spend the night at a resthouse built by the Direcção Regional de Turismo a few minutes from the sum-

Nature, always near on Madeira, runs from rugged to very gentle.

mit. Make arrangements in advance through the tourist office in Funchal. Whether you're there for the magnificent Atlantic sunrise or just during an average day, Pico Ruivo provides what must be Madeira's most spectacular **panorama.**

Ribeiro Frio (Cold Stream) is an uncommonly pleasant part of the countryside. The mountain brook from which the area takes its name maintains ever-fresh water in a government **trout hatchery.** In this model installation, you can watch the trout almost growing before your eyes. Across the road from the hatchery is a **botanical garden** designed to perpetuate every species of flower, plant and tree found on Madeira. The samples are labelled. Unlike Funchal's orderly botanical garden, the park at Ribeiro Frio sprawls unpredictably along twisting paths in a dark forest.

(Left) A guided tour for the very young; (right) Madeira's startlingly exotic flora.

This is an excellent place to explore Madeira's admirable system of **levadas**, irrigation channels. These watercourses, painfully built along cliffsides and around obstacles—Madeira has more than 600 miles of them—carry mountain spring water on the slightest gradient down to the fields which would otherwise be parched. Hundreds of years of audacious engineering work have saved the water; instead of roaring uselessly out to sea, it greens the terraces at all altitudes. Just north of the settlement of Ribeiro Frio, there's a path along the *levada*, which offers scenery and inspiration. Some tour operators organize guided hikes along the *levadas*.

SANTO DA SERRA is the usual abbreviation for the village of Santo António da Serra (St. Anthony of the Mountain). The altitude of more than 2,200 feet ensures refreshing breezes, explaining why so many well-to-do Madeirans hide out in villas here in the summer. The richly forested plateau enjoys a rare island attribute—flatness. The terrain is level enough for a nine-hole golf course, which is what the Santo da Serra Golf Club built here. If you're not a golfer, you'll still enjoy strolling through this territory, with its pines, eucalyptus and wild flowers.

Floating Garden

The metaphor about Madeira as a garden floating in the Atlantic will strike you as apt no matter what time of the year you arrive. Some delights to look for:

January
Flowering fields of *African daisies* as well as the swan-necked *Maguey plant*. Orchids blossom until May.

February
Hardy *tamarisk* and the *Abyssinian red hot poker* or *karat tree*.

March
Two from Brazil—the *cock's coral tree* (nature imitating nature) and the pastel-petalled *franciscea*.

April
Jacaranda blossoms into a cloud above Funchal's main avenue; elsewhere, see the delicately striped *painted trumpet*.

May
Flame tree flowers are fiery, but the *madonna*, or *white lily*, stays aloof.

June
On the hills, the purple-stalked *pride of Madeira*; and cheering roadsides, blue or white *agapanthus (African lily)*.

July
Hydrangea's light blue beauty is spontaneous; each *frangipani* petal looks hand-painted.

August
Cassia flowers in masses of cheerful yellow petals; even in blossom, the weird *dragon tree* looks as old as superstition itself.

September
From South Africa come creeping *podranea* and, in the hills, pink-and-white *belladonna lily*.

October
South American warmth in two sunny varieties—*golden trumpet* (or *allamanda*) and *stiverbush*.

November
Surprising red flowers of the *kaffir* or *lucky bean tree*; not just *daisies* but *daisy trees* full of them.

December
See in the New Year with flaming *poinsettia* and the vine variously called *golden shower* or *orange trumpet*.

And year-round the extravagant spectacle of *bougainvillea*, *mimosa*, *hibiscus* and the long-lasting *strelitzia*, or *bird-of-paradise* flower.

Excursions

🏃 Porto Santo

Area: 16 sq. miles
Pop. 5,000
(40 km. northeast of Madeira)

To Robinson Crusoe, Porto Santo would scarcely appear "undiscovered"; but the fact is that not so many tourists know of its charms. It's where the people of Madeira go on holiday to escape the crowds. The prime attraction, running almost the length of the island's south coast, is a perfect **sandy beach**, 5½ miles long. Apart from July, August and September, the only footprints you're likely to find in the sand are those of seagulls. But don't worry—if you stay on, there are some excellent hotel possibilities.

Once a day during the winter and three times daily in summer, a 244-passenger catamaran sails between Madeira and Porto Santo. The crossing takes about 1½ hours.

From the pier at the Porto de Abrigo, at the eastern tip of the island, it's a short bus or taxi ride, or a 15- to 20-minute walk, to the centre of
70 VILA BALEIRA*, the island's

only significant town. White walls, palms and scrub give the place something of a wild-west air. Neon signs and haste have barely been invented.

But if you're in a hurry, you'll save time flying instead of sailing from Madeira to Porto Santo. You'll obviously be paying a good deal more, however. There are daily flights to Porto Santo airport, which takes up a sizeable chunk of the centre of the island. The airfield is, in fact, nearly as long as the island is wide, and it's a reserve air base for NATO.

Aside from year-round swimming—the sand slopes gently into the ocean along a lengthy crescent—the scuba-diving and deep-sea fishing are rated very highly. Hunters take to the rocky hills for partridge and rabbit. It's said that the first colonists in 1418 brought with them a pair of rabbits, which multiplied so rapidly that for years the descendant rodents constituted a plague. Beyond the realm of outdoor sports there's frankly not much to do in Porto Santo.

Vila Baleira is its most

---

* The town is also referred to as Porto Santo.

PORTO SANTO

colourful self in August, with vivid feasts, juicy figs and grapes, and great yellow melons...and all the bubbly crowds of Madeiran tourists.

Towards sunset you'll want to sit in the main square and listen to the birds twittering in the branches of the palms. Then you have the choice of a few restaurants and bars, peace, silence, bliss.

There are occasional buses. Otherwise, you can walk or take a taxi for your sightseeing.

A taxi will drive you very nearly to the summit of PICO DO CASTELO (Castle Peak), a perfect volcanic cone 1,443 feet high. On a clear day you can see Madeira from the lookout point not far below the peak. A couple of rusted cannon on the peak (which is craterless and flat) show that it used to be a fortress and refuge from pirates. In the 16th and 17th centuries the beach was so inviting to buccaneers, and the defenders were so few, that the populace simply took to the hills when trouble arrived.

The island's highest peak is PICO DO FACHO, 1,663 feet. *Facho* means "torch". On this **72** peak sentries would light

torches to signal Madeira, warning that pirates had been sighted.

On the rugged north coast you can see a cliffside that seems to come right out of a geology textbook: at FONTE DA AREIA (Fountain of Sand) all the strata are plainly marked in colour. In some

places the wind has pock-marked the cliffside, creating many small caves. But they're uninhabited. The Fonte da Areia is also the source of Porto Santo's mineral water (see p. 77).

Elsewhere on the island many steep, rocky hills have been heroically terraced.

Madeira has its comprehensive irrigation system, but here the future of the crops depends entirely on rainfall. Wheat and grapes are the principal agricultural pro-

Columbus honeymooned in Vila Baleira, 'capital' of Porto Santo.

ducts. You can watch the wheat being threshed in the old-fashioned way; then taste the local bread, which is irresistible. You'll also appreciate the fresh fish, fruit and vegetables, while the grapes produce a remarkable, powerful wine. In appearance and taste it resembles Madeira wine, but the Porto Santo variety requires

Porto Santo's economy still turns on animal power and wind power. Opposite: view inside the mill grinding flour for the island's bread.

no complicated or lengthy production processes. It's just naturally hearty.

Another change from the Madeiran landscape: in many parts of Porto Santo you'll see cattle grazing. Picture a herd of cows silhouetted on a ridge with the ocean as a backdrop and a windmill in the foreground. Only a few windmills still function on Porto Santo; one or two are nicely situated for amateur photographers.

The sights of the island's capital, Vila Baleira, are modest. Chickens scratch for lunch within 100 yards of the town hall—a pleasant, old two-storey building. On the other side of the triangular main square is the island's principal church, begun in the 15th century. Behind the whitewashed church, Rua Cristóvão Colombo (Columbus Street) honours Porto Santo's most illustrious adopted son. Having married the daughter of Governor Bartolomeu Perestrelo, Columbus settled on the island, although not for long (see p. 14).

(see p. 14)

The corner house at Rua Colombo 8 used to be the local jail. Look in through the big barred door. The mismatched plasterwork on the ceiling testifies to one prisoner's successful escape. The two-storey house at Rua Colombo 12 is said to be the house in which Columbus lived. Whether or not he actually did is uncertain, although he undoubtedly would have seen very similar buildings all around.

The house, overshadowed by tall, shady palms, is now the Columbus House Museum.

The people of Porto Santo, who live close to the land with few luxuries, sometimes resent the wealth of their Madeiran cousins. For most *Portosantenses*, the life of farming or fishing has changed very little over the centuries. The islanders are still called *profetas* ("prophets") because of a 16th-century scandal: a local shepherd with a fertile imagination tricked everyone into joining a weird cult, to the dismay of the Catholic Church. But it was only a temporary aberration. Today almost everyone goes to mass on Sunday, and the only pagan cult known in the vicinity is sun worship. Some

Formidably spacious sandy beach sprawls along the south coast.

people say the sand of Porto Santo has curative properties. Others rave about the mineral water which is found on the island. It's bottled very near the centre of Vila Baleira and exported to appreciative customers on Madeira, deprived of minerals in their own drinking water.

If you can sacrifice the nightlife for a few days, Porto Santo is an Atlantic hideaway you should get to know.

More Islands

As flights from Lisbon approach Madeira they usually descend over three islands slinking off to the south-east, so grim and forbidding that the sight of Madeira's fertile hillsides comes as a considerable relief.

Navigational charts show that the Ilhas Desertas (Deserted Islands) are really an extension of Madeira, connected by a ridge of underwater mountains; nearly 11 miles of ocean separate the most northerly and smallest Deserta, called CHÃO, from the lighthouse at Ponta de São Lourenço. *Chão* means "level" and, indeed, from the south-east coast of Madeira this island looks like a small, flat tugboat pulling its two mountainous sisters through the Atlantic. DESERTA GRANDE and BUGIO are the names of the larger isles. All three are uninhabited except for birds and game.

In summer, boat trips can be organized individually to explore the inhospitable coasts of the Desertas. Landing is difficult, and the authorities on Madeira should be advised in advance.

Local observers report an

Atlantic sunset silhouettes palm trees on a Madeira hillside.

optical phenomenon: when the sky is perfectly clear you can't see the Desertas from Funchal. But with cloud or mist they immediately become visible. Sunsets reflect a fiery glow on the isles—when they can be seen.

Completing the roster of obscure islands making up the Madeira archipelago are the rocky ILHAS SELVAGENS, or "savage islands". Almost nobody from Madeira has ever seen the Selvagens, which are closer to the Canary Islands than to any Portuguese territory. There are two principal islands and several islets and reefs with a total area of less than one and a half square miles. Like the Desertas, the Selvagens are uninhabited and uninviting.

What to Do

Shopping

The talent of the local artisans is what makes shopping so rewarding on Madeira. From cheap souvenirs to considerable works of folk art, the island's products bear the imprint of distinctive craftsmanship. However, don't expect bargains in cameras, radios or whisky; that's the domain of the duty-free ports, such as those tropical Caribbean islands. (With or without taxes, you'll enjoy shopping in Madeira.)

Where to Shop

Funchal's business district has the best variety of shops and products. Additionally, there are smaller boutiques or branches of Funchal establishments in and around the major hotels. You can also visit handiwork factories to watch how wicker or embroidery are made, with the option (but without the obligation) to buy. Wine-tasting at wine shops will help you choose the type of Madeira wine to take home. If all else fails, surrender to the impulse and patronize the salesmen hawking souvenirs at key tourist locations. And if you can't make up your mind until the last moment, there are souvenir shops at the check-in level of the airport.

Of course, the wise shopper goes about it methodically and without haste, comparing quality and prices in several places before buying even the most trifling item.

Shopping hours are 9 a.m. to 1 p.m. and 3 to 7 p.m., Monday to Friday; 9 a.m. to 1 p.m. only on Saturday. Shopping centres are open from 9.30 a.m. to 10 p.m. (although some shops close as early as 7 p.m.) daily, including Saturdays, Sundays and holidays.

An ABC of What to Buy

Azulejos. Hand-decorated glazed tiles, often in traditional blue and white, sometimes copies of antique designs; a Portuguese speciality for 400 years, but not at all easy to find in Madeira.

Bolo de mel. Delicious, long-lasting Madeiran molasses cake, packed for export.

Boots. Souvenir versions of the traditional island footwear, knee-high but worn rolled down to the ankle. **79**

Bottles. Filled with Madèira wine or *aguardente* (liquor); or sets of bottles, big and small, packed for carrying past the eyes of admiring customs inspectors.

Carved models. Primarily sailing-boats of modern or historic design.

Embroidery. Table linen, sheets, dresses, blouses, handkerchiefs. Embroidered by thousands of Madeiran women, either at home in the countryside or in factories in Funchal, where they can be seen working on the detailed and exquisite patterns.

Flowers. Orchids, strelitzia (bird-of-paradise) or other tropical beauties, specially wrapped to be carried onto your plane.

Glassware. Including the

A flower vendor displays her wares in Funchal centre.

narrow-stemmed glasses out of which experts say madeira wine should be drunk.

Hand-painted items. Ashtrays, paperweights and similar mementoes for budget-conscious holiday-makers.

Marquetry. A recently revived craft: pictures, boxes and other small items as well as desks and tables; mainly found in Funchal's Old Town.

Musical instruments. You can buy a guitar, a flute

or—what could be more typically Madeiran?—a *brinquinho*, the percussion instrument adorned with dancing dolls.

Porcelain, pottery. Plates, platters, figurines, jugs, jars, all brightly hand-painted.

Roosters. Cheerful statues in all sizes, modelled in ceramics or carved out of wood. Recalling the rooster on the judge's dinner plate which got up and crowed to prove the innocence of a doomed defendant; or so goes the legend in the northern Portuguese town of Barcelos, where the cockerel first became the nation's symbol.

Straw hats. Old-fashioned boaters and miniature models, as well as bonnets, sombreros and many others.

Tapestry. Another Madeiran outlet for nimblefingered needle-workers; production emphasizes copies of famous paintings.

Wickerwork. A serious branch of the export trade, based on a cottage industry. Trays and boxes, chairs and tables, plus model ships and animal figures. All handmade, of course.

Wool. Rugs and blankets in unusual colours and patterns. Or you can buy a colourful souvenir variety of **81**

Gifts for all tastes, from intricate wicker baskets to cheerful embroidery.

the Madeiran workman's woollen cap with pompom and earflaps.

Wrought-ironwork. If the overweight baggage problem doesn't bother you. Pot-holders, book-ends and heavier objects in the tradition of a notable Portuguese folk-art.

Folklore

By a municipal edict of 1933, all the women who sell flowers in Funchal must wear the native costume of Madeira on the job. You can get a good look at the cheerful colours in the little plaza alongside the cathedral and also at the city market.

Younger girls wear the same red-and-yellow striped skirts with (usually) red bolero jacket, red cape and boots at demonstrations of Madeiran music and dance. It's worth seeing the dancing groups when they come to your hotel or join one of the folklore-at-sea boating excursions scheduled for fine evenings.

Skirts used to be voluminous to conceal the long white bloomers beneath, but modern fashions have prevailed—some are now mini-length. Onlookers are invited to join in, or to clap, as the performers twirl through the energetic square dances, accompanied by the island's equivalent of hillbilly music.

The men's costumes consist of white linen suits with red cummerbunds and waistcoats, and curious black skull-caps with slim tassels standing up like candlewicks.

Both men and women wear the native boots, called *botachã* (literally "plain boot"). At first glance they look like Eskimo *mukluks*. They're made of tanned oxhide and goatskin, with a narrow red band around the part which is rolled down to the ankle.

Except for a standard accordion, the musical instruments are uniquely Madeiran. A guitar-like stringed instrument called a *machête* is plunked in what may strike you as a monotonous couple of chords. A drum and a triangle set the rhythm, but the most extraordinary percussion instrument is the *brinquinho*, constructed of tiny costumed dolls dancing around a maypole. This contraption adds oriental overtones to the songs.

The music and dances tell stories going back to the earliest Madeiran times. They evoke harvest rituals, grapecrushing and the formalities of courtship, usually to the tune of a light two-step. Hand-clapping and finger-snapping accompany some of the dances.

For a change of pace from Madeira's folklore, you'll enjoy the more sophisticated music of the *fado*, the most popular type of song of main- **83**

Festivals

Fascinating local festivals occur throughout the island at all times of the year. But the most spectacular celebrations are concentrated at the end of December.

Elaborate preparations always precede Christmas—decorating the streets, baking *bolo de mel* (the rich molasses cake), cooking the year's most sumptuous feasts. Special displays of flowers, fruit and vegetables attract crowds to Funchal's municipal market and the nearby streets. All the churches are packed for midnight mass.

New Year's Eve on Madeira has acquired a worldwide reputation for gaiety and light. The itineraries of winter cruises in the Atlantic are arranged so as to allow a stop at Funchal on December 31. At midnight the view from a harbour anchorage is unforgettable, but those ashore can share in the spectacle as the hills above Funchal come ablaze in a fantastic firework display, accompanied by the peal of church

land Portugal. The tunes are often, though not necessarily, sad. They tend to concentrate on human tragedies, hopelessness and destiny, hence the name *fado* (fate). The singer, sometimes a woman, is accompanied by a couple of guitars; their complex chords approximate the lush sound of a zither. You can hear *fado* performed in Madeiran nightclubs or as part of the folklore presentations.

84

Brightly costumed dancers swing to the rhythm of a brinquinho.

bells and the blast of ships' whistles and sirens.

Among the religious festivals during the rest of the year, one in particular stands out. This is the Feast of the Assumption, known in Madeira more parochially as the Festival of Nossa Senhora do Monte (Our Lady of the Mount) and fervently celebrated on August 14 and 15 in the village of Monte. Pilgrims come from all parts of the island to kiss the image of Madeira's patron saint in the specially decorated parish church. Loudspeakers relaying the service to crowds outside compete with the din of ice-cream salesmen and megaphones luring country folk to wheels of chance.

Some other local festivals on the calendar:

June 23-24: Funchal, São João da Ribeira.

June 28-30: Ribeira Brava, São Pedro.

Sept. (1st Sun.): Ponta Delgada, Senhor Jesus.

Sept. 7-8: Calheta, Nossa Senhora do Loreto.

Sept. 9: Machico, Nosso Senhor dos Milagres.

Visitors will also enjoy the annual carnival parade (February), flower show (April), motor rally (August) and wine festival (September).

Nightlife

The major hotels of western Funchal make up the nucleus of the nightlife scene. Their cocktail lounges, discotheques and night-clubs have inspired clusters of local bars and dives to throb in the same neighbourhood. But holiday-makers in other parts of the island needn't be isolated. The big tourist complexes have their own diversions right on the premises, with a full agenda of music, dancing and floorshows.

Casino: Funchal's casino, part of an architectural complex designed by Oscar Niemeyer (of Brasília fame) is open from 8 p.m. to 3 a.m. (closed on Mondays). Gambling possibilities include roulette, chemin-de-fer, blackjack and slot machines. A moderate fee is charged for admission. You must hand over your passport for registration formalities.

Museums

Museu de Arte Sacra, Rua do Bispo. 15th- and 16th-century Portuguese and Flemish art (see p. 27).

Museu Municipal, Rua da Mouraria; aquarium and na-

Fearful specimen intrigues young visitors to the Museu Municipal.

tural history museum (see pp. 31–32).

Firemen's Museum, Caminho de Dom João. Equipment and curiosities relating to the history of firefighting in Madeira.

Photographia Museu "Vicente", Avenida Zarco. Interesting photo studio museum with 19th-century cameras, glass plates, negatives.

Casa-Museu Frederico de Freitas, Calçada de Santa Clara. Madeira scenes by 19th-century English artists; sculptures; antique furniture; ceramics.

Museu Henrique & Francisco Franco, Rua João de Deus. Sculptures and paintings by the Franco brothers, the island's best known artists of the 1920s and '30s.

Museu de Cidade do Funchal. Municipal history (see page 25).

Quinta das Cruzes, Calçada do Pico 7. Finely furnished 15th-century villa and surrounding garden with archaeological display (see pp. 31-32).

Local art on view in villa-turned-museum, Quinta das Cruzes.

Sightseeing Tours

Several firms run coach tours covering most of the essential sights of the island. The excursions are divided into one-day or half-day outings totalling about a week's worth of sightseeing. Pamphlets listing the itineraries and prices can be found at hotel reception desks, where you can reserve seats on the tours. Passengers are picked up and delivered to their hotels. On full-day excursions you can take a box lunch or sign up in advance for a restaurant meal. No coach excursion covers all the highlights in a single day, so if time is scarce you'll have to decide whether you prefer mountains or seascapes, or would like to examine local folklore and handicrafts.

Other companies operate boat trips according to a varied schedule covering the sights near Funchal as well as all-day outings with swimming included. When the sea is calm, the boats ease close to shore so you can look down on the giant boulders paving the ocean floor here. Notice how the coastline alternates between rich, terraced farmland and stark basalt cliffs.

Sports and Other Activities

Surrounded by the Atlantic Ocean, Madeira naturally puts the emphasis on aquatic sports, from plain old-fashioned swimming to scuba-diving and deep-sea fishing. But you can turn your back on the sea and participate in landlocked sports as vigorous as tennis or mountain-climbing. For the rare but inevitable rainy day, you can keep active with billiards or table-tennis.

Water, water everywhere: hotel's swimming pool overlooks Atlantic.

Swimming

Most of the coast of Madeira runs steeply into the sea, but where there are bays and harbours the beaches tend to boulders or shingle. As for sandy beaches, the only one, Praínha, is in an isolated position towards the eastern tip of the island. (For sandy-beach fans an excursion to neighbouring Porto Santo island will relieve any frustration.)

Several major hotels in Funchal have their own swimming facilities along the difficult shoreline, making it possible to get into and out of the sea without trouble. Similar arrangements have been made by private clubs and the municipality.

Funchal's Lido, a massive swimming-pool complex along the coast towards Ponta da Cruz, provides facilities for 2,300 bathers, along with solariums, restaurants and bars.

Natural, or mostly-natural, swimming pools protected by rock formations permit sea swimming in vulnerable locations: Porto Moniz and Ponta Delgada.

Otherwise, all big hotels have their own swimming pools, often with seawater warmed in chilly seasons.

Undersea Exploration

The clear blue sea surrounding Madeira abounds in fish and interesting vegetation; around the coast, tiny bays and underwater caverns stir the sense of adventure. For a superficial look, you can buy a mask and snorkel tube at one of the shops. For exploration in depth, scuba equipment and launches can be hired. The Direcção Regional de Turismo, the official tourist office at Avenida Arriaga 16–18, Funchal, has details of underwater sightseeing and fishing.

Sailing, Boating

A private firm, operating out of the Lido, has sailing boats, kayaks and sailboards for hire. Or try the Direcção Regional de Desportes. Guests of the luxury hotels have their own facilities.

Water-Skiing, Windsurfing

Several hotels have their own motorboats and water skis, and there are plenty of facilities for windsurfing.

Sports for everyone: fishermen and swimmer share the ocean.

Fishing from Shore
Drop a line over the side from the Funchal jetty or anywhere else which strikes your fancy. Sea bream, sea perch, grey mullet, moray eel and conger eel await your bait.

Deep-Sea Fishing
You might not break the Madeiran (and European) record of a 1,212-pound marlin, or spearfish, but big ones by any standard are pulled in every day. If the marlin are shy, you have a chance of catching tunny (tuna), swordfish and shark. Regular excursions are advertised by the firms operating at the Funchal *cais*. You can also ask the tourist office how you can organize a private outing.

Sports Ashore

Mini-golf
There are several mini-links —guaranteed to please young and old alike.

Golf
Tourists are invited to play the Santo da Serra golf course 30 kilometres northeast of Funchal (gradually being extended to a projected 27 holes). Green fees are higher at weekends and on public holidays.

Tennis
The principal hotels, tourist complexes and clubs have their own courts. Professional instruction is available at most large hotels. Squash is also played at some.

Hunting
October to December is the season for rabbit, partridge, quail and pigeon on Madeira. The tourist office has details of how to obtain licences.

Hiking
Whether you yearn to climb Madeira's highest mountain (Pico Ruivo, 6,105 feet) or just go for an hour's ramble through wild ferns and flowers, there are quite a few specific, recommended walks.

Other Sports
Hotels and clubs offer a range of other activities: skeet- or trap-shooting, billiards, table-tennis, bridge and chess, for example.

By way of spectator sports, Madeirans lean heavily towards football (soccer).

You can also watch basketball, volleyball and hockey matches.

Wining and Dining

There's no shortage of elegant eating places on Madeira. After all, wealthy foreign visitors have been catered for since Victorian times. Nonetheless, if your taste or budget should lean towards unaffected local food instead of *haute cuisine*, no problem will arise.

Be ready for one surprise, though. If you've been resigned to eating plastic mass-produced food at home, your taste buds will rejoice in the freshness of Madeira's fruit, vegetables, fish, eggs, butter and bread. Many of the flavours are so authentic you may have forgotten how good they are.

A shady café—just the place to plan your sightseeing strategy.

Choosing a Restaurant

Government inspectors rate all Portuguese restaurants according to four categories. In descending order, they are: *de luxu* (luxury), *de primeira*, *de segunda* and *de terceira classe* (first-, second- and third-class). The higher the rating the more the restaurant is permitted to charge. Menus are put up in the window or just beside the door so you know what to expect in variety and price. Look for the *prato do dia* (day's speciality), which may be the cook's favourite dish. All restaurant prices include a service charge but an additional tip is appreciated.

Meal Times

Breakfast (*o pequeno almoço*) is eaten any time until about 10 a.m. Lunch (*o almoço*) is served from noon to 3 p.m. Dinner (*o jantar*) runs from about 7 to 10 p.m. Some restaurants offer all-day service from morning until midnight, and some places serve until 2 a.m. Between meals you can also have a snack

A sumptuous array to set your tastebuds tingling. Right: maître d'hôtel puts last touches to delicate fish dish.

at a *pastelaria* (pastry and cake shop) or a substantial amount of food at a snack bar. (The Portuguese word is *snack-bar*.)

Breakfast
The Portuguese usually begin the day with coffee, toast or a roll, butter and jam. (The home-made jams of Madeira cover an inventive and delicious range from apple and apricot to mango and tomato.) Hotels can provide orange juice, eggs, bacon or whatever else is required to imitate an English or American breakfast.

The Madeira Gourmet
Life is simple in the countryside of Madeira. The diet stresses fish, fruit and vegetables; except at Christmastime, the country people seldom eat meat.

But the spartan regime doesn't extend to the restaurants. You'll find an ample variety of food, including tasty chicken, pork and veal dishes. They're served with ample helpings of rice, potatoes and fresh cooked vegetables.

*For more information on wining and dining in Portugal, consult the Berlitz EUROPEAN MENU READER.

In the major hotels you can order from an international menu or concentrate on Portuguese dishes.*

First, a look at some regional delicacies from Madeira:

Caldo verde: a variation of the "green broth" that originated in northern Portugal, this is essentially a soup of cabbage and potatoes, including a slice of sausage.

Espada: Madeira's ubiquitous fish is big enough to fil-

Especially Confusing

A menu in any foreign language can be difficult, but Madeira poses unique problems. Don't let these troublesome words, all beginning with the letters esp, "espoil" your appetite:

espada: scabbard fish, or cutlass fish

espadarte: swordfish

espargos: asparagus

espetada: skewered beef

espinafres: spinach

It's all quite *espantoso* — astonishing.

let into several hearty helpings. It's poached in wine, then breaded and grilled or simmered with spices and vegetables.

Bife de atum: steak of another local fish, tunny (tuna), grilled and served with lemon and the usual large helpings of rice, potatoes and vegetables.

Espetada: skewered beef with a top-secret ingredient—the scent of the fire over which the kebabs are grilled; fragrant twigs of laurel must be used to kindle the flames. Madeirans love the do-it-yourself *espetada* parties accompanying all local festivals.

Milho: a mainstay in the local diet, maize-meal (corn-meal) is used in several ways—as an element in soup, a substitute for bread or as a polenta side-dish.

Inhame: a kind of sweet potato. Popular as a vegetable on its own or fried with ordinary potatoes to make mixed chips, or french fries.

Pudim: a slice of caramel mould steeped in a Madeira wine sauce.

Bolo de mel: a rich, dark molasses cake with cinnamon, fruits and nuts. Traditionally, Madeira's Christmas treat but you can eat it at any time.

Fresh fruit: in addition to all the familiar fruit grown on Madeira—apples, bananas, cherries, figs, grapes, lemons, oranges, plums and strawberries—you'll want to investigate the more exotic tropical items such as guava, mango, papaya and passionfruit. Look for the succulent melons brought over from Porto Santo.

Portuguese Cuisine

Cooks in continental Portugal have a reputation for devising ingenious variations on seafood dishes. You'll come across these and other mainland specialities on the menus of Madeira:

Sopa de grão: chick-pea soup enhanced with tomato and onion.

Canja: chicken-and-rice soup.

Caldeirada: a rich, slowly simmered fish soup with onions, potatoes and olive oil.

Bacalhau à Gomes de Sá: one of the hundreds of ways the Portuguese cook cod, the national fish. In this recipe they add olives, onions, garlic and hard-boiled eggs.

Bife de cebolada: steak braised in a wine and onion sauce.

Cozido à Portuguesa: a stew of beef, pork, sausage, rice and vegetables.

Arroz de frango: chicken, rice and optional meat and sauce.

Coelho assado: roast rabbit with onion and spices.

Table Wine
Most Madeiran restaurants serve table wine originating in continental Portugal. Here are a few of the better-known types:

Almeirim: white wines with a high alcohol content.

Unlovely though tasty, espada is featured at Funchal fish market.

Amaxante: red wine, similar to *vinho verde.*

Bairrada: red, white and sparkling wines.

Bucelas: dry, white wines.

Carcavelos: powerful, distinctive wines.

Colares: aromatic red wine.

Dão: ruby reds and refreshing whites.

Pinhel: light rosé.

Vinho Verde: "green wine" —from unripe grapes—produced in northern Portugal, light and sparkling in red and white versions.

Table wine from Madeira: a rich, fruity red wine, not produced for export. Not to be confused with the before and after-dinner wines known, simply, as Madeira.

Madeira Wine

The famous *vinho generoso,* the aged and blended wine of Madeira, has been a royal favourite for centuries. It comes in four varieties:

Sercial, a lush, dry aperitif, reminiscent of sherry

Verdelho, medium-dry, amber-coloured, subtly flavoured

Boal, or *Bual,* a fragrant, semi-sweet dessert wine.

Malvasia (Malmsey) mellow, full-bodied dessert wine with unblemished country taste.

Other Beverages

Lager beers come in various brands, brewed locally, shipped from mainland Portugal or imported from other European countries.

It's perfectly safe to drink tap water, but Madeirans often order bottled mineral

Determined study will make these visitors expert on Madeira wines.

water from Porto Santo for its fizz and mineral content. Tonic, cola and similar soft drinks in local and international brands are widely available; also bottled fruit juice.

Maracujá is a distinctively Madeiran bottled refresher resembling a fizzy lemonade but made of the pulp of passion-fruit.

Liquor
Aguardente is locally distilled rum, a powerful potion, suitable for theoretical snakebite crises. Enthusiasts find the liquor warms the blood when drunk in one gulp. *Aguardente* can also mean any kind of liquor.

Coffee
Madeirans aren't nearly as addicted to coffee as their cousins in Brazil, who seem to be sipping *cafezinhos* all day long. But espresso machines are found in a great many bars and restaurants. If the Madeiran coffee is too strong or unfamiliar, you can order instant coffee instead. Just say, "Um nescafé". A white coffee is known on Madeira as a *Chineses*. (Chinese Lady.)

To Help You Order...

Could we have a table?
Do you have a set menu?
I'd like a/an/some...

Queríamos uma mesa.
Tem uma ementa turística?
Queria...

beer	uma cerveja	mineral water	água mineral
bread	pão	napkin	um guardanapo
coffee	um café	pepper	pimenta
condiments	temperos	potatoes	batatas
cutlery	talheres	rice	arroz
dessert	uma sobremesa	salad	uma salada
fish	peixe	salt	sal
fruit	fruta	sandwich	uma sanduíche
glass	um copo	soup	uma sopa
ice-cream	um gelado	sugar	açúcar
meat	carne	tea	chá
menu	a ementa	(iced) water	água (fresca)
milk	leite	wine	vinho

... and Read the Menu

alho	garlic	**guisado**	stew
almôndegas	meatballs	**hors-d'oeuvre**	hors-d'oeuvre
alperces	apricots	**lagosta**	spiny lobster
ameijoas	baby clams	**lagostins**	prawns
ananaz	pineapple	**laranja**	orange
arroz	rice	**legumes**	vegetables
assado	roast	**limão**	lemon
atum	tunny (tuna)	**linguado**	sole
azeitonas	olives	**lombo**	fillet
bacalhau	codfish	**lulas**	squid
banana	banana	(à sevilhana)	(deep-fried)
besugo	sea bream	**maçãs**	apple
bife (vaca)	beef steak	**mariscos**	shellfish
biscoitos/	biscuits	**melancia**	watermelon
bolachas	(cookies)	**mexilhões**	mussels
bolo	cake	**molho**	sauce
borrego	lamb	**morangos**	strawberries
caracóis	snails	**omelete**	omelette
caranguejo	crab	**ostras**	oysters
cavala	mackerel	**ovo**	egg
cebola	onions	**peixe**	fish
chouriço	a spicy	**pescada**	hake
	sausage	**pescadinha**	whiting
coelho	rabbit	**pêssego**	peach
cogumelos	mushrooms	**pimento**	green pepper
costeletas	chops	**polvos**	baby octopus
dobrada	tripe	pequenos	
dourada	sea-bass	**porco**	pork
enguias	eel	**presunto**	ham
ervilhas	peas	**queijo**	cheese
feijões	beans	**romãs**	pomegranates
figos	figs	**salada**	salad
filete	fish fillet	**salmonetes**	red mullet
flã	caramel	**salsichão**	salami
	mould	**sobremesa**	dessert
framboesas	raspberries	**sopa**	soup
frango	chicken	**torrada**	toast
frito	fried	**truta**	trout
gambas	shrimp	**uvas**	grapes
100 **gelado**	ice-cream	**vitela**	veal

BLUEPRINT for a Perfect Trip

How to Get There

Because of the complexity and variability of the many fares, you should ask the advice of an informed travel agent well before departure.

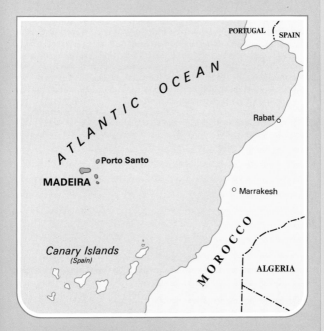

From the United Kingdom

BY AIR: There are several direct and nonstop services from London to Funchal each week in the peak summer months. There are also daily connections to Funchal from Lisbon, a 1½ hour flight. Out of season, flights operate on a reduced schedule. Excursion fares are offered that provide considerable savings over the normal economy return fare. To qualify, you must stay in Madeira for between six days and a month.

Charter Flights and Package Tours: The package tour—with flight, hotel and meals included—remains a popular way of visiting Madeira and is usually the cheapest.

BY SEA: A good number of tour operators include Madeira on their cruiseship itineraries. Usually, the visit is of a short duration—perhaps only an overnight stop for shopping and brief sightseeing.

Potential voyagers from Britain seeking only a sea passage without the frills of an organized cruise should ask their travel agent about freighter sailings for Funchal. Cargo vessels, with limited passenger accommodation, leave at quite frequent intervals.

Small cargo ships sail at least weekly between Lisbon and Funchal. It's a two-day trip, and cabin accommodation is available. It's possible to have your car put aboard. Space for cars and passengers, is, of course, limited, so that it's wise to book your passage early.

From North America

BY AIR: Regular services operate to Funchal from New York, Boston and Montreal, via Lisbon—though not always daily. The summer schedule offers more choice. Check with your travel agent for current flight information.

On scheduled flights, significant economies can be made if plans can be completed far enough in advance and certain other requirements are met.

When to Go

Madeira's climate is most famous for its winter warmth. Though the winter months are relatively wet and the winds get noticeably stronger, the weather remains agreeably warm. The rainiest period is from October to December, with an average of 6 to 7 days of rain per month—but you can still usually count on an average of 6 hours of sunshine a day.

In summer, from May to September, the air is warm and a little humid. Rain falls mainly in the mountains. At sea level, clouds often form in the afternoons, but Funchal still has an average of 7 hours of sunshine a day.

Air and sea temperatures in Funchal:

		J	F	M	A	M	J	J	A	S	O	N	D
average daily	°F	56	56	56	58	60	63	66	67	67	65	61	58
minimum*	°C	13	13	13	14	16	17	19	19	19	18	16	14
average daily	°F	66	65	66	67	69	72	75	76	76	74	71	67
maximum*	°C	19	18	19	19	21	22	24	24	24	23	22	19
sea temperature	°F	63	63	63	63	64	66	68	70	72	73	68	64
(average monthly)	°C	17	17	17	17	18	19	20	21	22	23	20	18

*Minimum temperatures are measured just before sunrise, maximum temperatures in the early afternoon.

Planning Your Budget

To give you an idea of what to expect, here are some average prices in Portuguese escudos. However, all prices must be regarded as approximate, as inflation creeps relentlessly up.

Airport transfer. Public bus to Funchal 225 esc., taxi 2,500 esc. (20% higher between 10 p.m. and 6 a.m.).

Baby-sitters. 1,500 esc. per hour. Transport home after midnight.

Bus. Funchal–Câmara de Lobos 130 esc., Funchal–Monte 145 esc., Funchal–Machico 145 esc., local trips in Funchal 145 esc.

Car hire (international company; all prices with unlimited mileage). *Opel Corsa* 5,400 esc. a day, 50,400 esc. per week. *Renault Clio* 4,800 esc. a day, 63,000 esc. per week. *Minibus* (for 9 people) 12,000 esc. a day, 80,000 esc. per week. Add 12% tax.

Cigarettes. Portuguese brands from 200 esc., imported brands from 300 esc.

Entertainment. Casino night club 600 esc., cinema 350 esc.

Guides. 9,000 esc. for half-day, 16,000 esc. per day (50% extra Sundays).

Hairdressers. *Woman's* haircut 1,300 esc., permanent wave 4,500 esc. *Man's* haircut from 700 esc.

Hotels (double room with bath per night). ***** 40,000 esc., **** 28,000 esc., *** 15,000 esc., ** 9,000 esc.

Meals and drinks. Lunch/dinner in fairly good establishment 2,500 esc., coffee 100 esc., Portuguese brandy up to 350 esc., bottle of beer 125 esc., soft drink 100 esc., liqueur/Madeira from 160 esc., bottle of wine from 250 esc.

Sports. Scuba diving 10,000 esc. per dive with equipment, 4,000 esc. without equipment, golf green fee 2,000 esc., caddies 500 esc., clubs 1,500 esc., tennis 250–1,000 esc. per hour.

104 **Taxi.** Excursions: 5,000 esc. for half-day, 10,000 esc. per day.

An A–Z Summary of Practical Information and Facts

A star (*) following an entry indicates that relevant prices are to be found on page 104.
  Listed after some basic entries is the appropriate Portuguese translation, usually in the singular, plus a number of phrases that should help you when seeking assistance.

AIRPORT *(aeroporto)*. Madeira's Santa Catarina airport lies 22 kilo- **A** metres north-east of Funchal. The modern airport building is equipped with souvenir stands, a duty-free shop, a currency-exchange office, bar, restaurant and car-rental facilities. There are no porters to help passengers with luggage; free hand-trolleys are provided instead.
  On the neighbouring island of Porto Santo, the airport has been operating since 1960—four years before Madeira's was completed. But in spite of its international-class runway, sometimes used for NATO air manoeuvres, Porto Santo is primarily a local stop on the national Portuguese airline (TAP) timetable.

Taxi!	**Táxi**
Where's the bus for ...?	**Onde é o autocarro para...?**

BABY-SITTERS. Most hotels organize baby-sitting at short notice. **B** You may be charged extra for the hours after midnight and for the sitter's transport home. In out-of-the-way spots somebody's grand- mother may have to be recruited.

Can you get me a baby-sitter for tonight?	**Pode encontrar-me uma baby-sitter para esta noite?**

BICYCLES. Put aside the idea of renting a bike to see the scenery up close. Madeira's countryside is so hilly and the roads so bumpy that cycling is almost exclusively the sport of serious racers.
  On Porto Santo, however, it is a perfectly realizable and enjoyable possibility.

C **CAMPING.** There are campsites at Porto Moniz, Ponta do Sol and Santa da Serra. On Porto Santo, there's a large camping ground on the beach just outside Vila Baleira.

CAR HIRE* *(carros de aluguer)*. International and local car-hire firms operate in Funchal and major tourist areas. At certain seasons, the demand for cars may exceed the supply, making it necessary to book several days in advance. In addition to the usual drive-yourself cars, chauffeur service is available.

This being a small island, unlimited mileage is included in the charge, but the customer must pay for the fuel. A tax is added to the bill. Third-party insurance is included in the basic charge but you must pay an extra fee for collision-damage waiver policy and personal accident insurance.

You must have a valid driving licence with at least a year's driving experience. The minimum age for hiring a car is generally 23 (21 for some firms). If you present a recognized credit card the deposit will be waived.

I'd like to hire a car today/tomorrow.	**Queria alugar um carro para hoje/amanhã.**
for one day/a week	**por um dia/uma semana**
Please include full insurance.	**Inclua um seguro contra todos os riscos, por favor.**

CIGARETTES, CIGARS, TOBACCO* *(cigarros, charutos, tabaco)*. Cigarettes imported from Europe and the United States cost about three times more than the Portuguese product on Madeira. Among local brands—manufactured on the island—are *Magos, EM, Boaviagem, Bingo* and *Goldflame.*

Tobacco shops sell Portuguese and foreign cigars and pipe tobacco as well.

Smoking is prohibited in theatres and cinemas, indoor sports areas and local buses.

A packet of cigarettes/matches.	**Um maço de cigarros/fósforos.**
filter-tipped	**com filtro**
without filter	**sem filtro**
light tobacco	**tabaco amarelo**
dark tobacco	**tabaco castanho**

CLOTHING. Clothes suitable for the sunny climate are the order of the day, year-round, but there are seasonal variations. It can feel tropically hot some summer days; in winter you'll need a wrap for the evening. And don't forget the geographical complexity of a small, steep island: even if there's swimming in Funchal in December, snow may—though only rarely—cover the island's highest mountaintops. So you'll have to dress very warmly for expeditions to higher altitudes. And any time of year you'll want comfortable walking shoes, even for town strolling: the cobbled streets may be attractive but they're cruel on pampered feet.

Daytime dress is informal everywhere but a degree of formality is customary in the evenings, varying with the season and the hotel. With Funchal's upper crust, dressing for dinner is the habit.

Will I need a tie?	**É preciso gravata?**
Is it all right if I wear this?	**Vou bem assim?**

COMMUNICATIONS. Post offices are indicated by letters CTT *(Correios, Telégrafos e Telefones)*. If the post office is crowded or closed, you can buy stamps at many shops, such as tobacconists or souvenir stands. They usually display a sign, *Correios*. Most mailboxes on the street follow the British pillar-box design; they're painted red, too.

Hours. The main post office in Funchal operates from 8.30 a.m. to 8 p.m., Monday to Friday and 9 a.m. to 12.30 p.m. on Saturdays (same times as the post office on Avenida Zarco). Branch post offices work shorter hours.

Poste restante (general delivery). If you're uncertain of your holiday address, you may have letters sent to you care of the local post office – *posta restante*. For example:

> Mr. John Smith
> Posta Restante
> Funchal-Madeira
> Portugal

Be sure to take your passport or identity card when you go to pick up your letters from the *posta restante* window at the post office.

Telegrams *(telegrama)* can be sent from post offices, or you can give the text to your hotel receptionist. You may also send telegrams abroad through the Marconi Company, on Avenida Arriaga, near the

C cathedral, open seven days a week from 9 a.m. to midnight. Many hotels and post offices have telex facilities and will transmit and receive messages for their guests.

Telephone *(telefone)*. Most towns have automatic telephones in locations along the street. Deposit a 10-escudo coin for a local call. You'll also need 20- and 50-escudo coins. If you want to talk longer, you'll have to quickly insert another coin or you'll be cut off; unused ones are returned. However, more and more public telephones require a special card, *Credifone,* like a credit card, available from post office, which is sold in "conversation units" of 25 or 100, and which is replacing the old phone system. In cafés and restaurants, the telephones usually have meters and you pay so much per unit. You can make international telephone calls through the clerk at any post office or at your hotel. Be prepared for lengthy delays in summer.

Telephone Spelling Code							
A	Aveiro	H	Horta	O	Ovar	V	Vidago
B	Braga	I	Itália	P	Porto	W	Waldemar
C	Coimbra	J	José	Q	Queluz	X	Xavier
D	Dafundo	K	Kodak	R	Rossio	Y	York
E	Évora	L	Lisboa	S	Setúbal	Z	Zulmira
F	Faro	M	Maria	T	Tavira		
G	Guarda	N	Nazaré	U	Unidade		

Have you received any mail for...?	**Tem correio para...?**
A stamp for this letter/postcard, please.	**Um selo para esta carta/este postal, por favor.**
express (special delivery)	**expresso**
I want to send a telegram to...	**Quero mandar um telegrama para...**
Can you get me this number?	**Pode ligar-me para este número?**
reverse-charge (collect) call	**paga pelo destinatário**
person-to-person (personal) call	**com pré-aviso**

COMPLAINTS. If you've had no satisfaction from the manager of the shop, hotel or restaurant concerned, take your complaint straight to the tourist office. In any case, no other agency deals with these problems. If you have documents to support your claim, be sure to take them along.

CONSULATES and EMBASSIES *(consulado; embaixada)*. Several countries maintain consular offices in Funchal. For serious matters, people are usually referred to the embassy in Lisbon.

American Consular Agency: Avenida Luís de Camôes, Block D, Apartment B; tel.: 4 74 29.

British Consular Agency*: Avenida Zarco, 2; tel.: 2 12 21.

Lisbon embassies

Australia: Avenida da Liberdade, 244; tel. 52 33 50.

Canada: Rua Rosa Araújo, 2; tel. 56 38 21.

Eire: Rua da Impresa a Estrella, 1; tel. 66 15 69.

South Africa: Avenida Luís Bivar, 10; tel. 53 50 41.

United Kingdom: Rua S. Domingos à Lapa, 37; tel. 66 11 91.

U.S.A.: Avenida Forças Amadas, 16; tel. 72 66 00.

Where's the British/American consulate?	**Onde é o Consulado inglês/ americano?**

CONVERTER CHARTS. For fluid and distance measure, see page 111 Madeira, like the rest of Portugal, uses the metric system.

Temperature

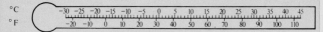

Length

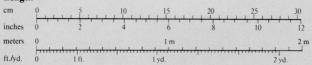

Weight

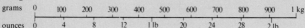

---

* Also for citizens of Commonwealth countries.

C **CRIME and THEFT.** Islands are rarely conducive to major crime, if only because the getaway is too difficult. But pick-pockets and petty larcenists occasionally try their hand on Madeira's tourists. Be careful with your wallet in crowds. It's also wise to keep your valuables in the hotel's safe. Report any theft to the hotel receptionist, the nearest police station or the police section in the tourist office.

I want to report a theft.   **Quero participar um roubo.**

D **DRIVING ON MADEIRA**

Shipping your car: It's a long and expensive project, rarely undertaken by holiday-makers. Check first with your automobile club, but you will need a national driving licence (valid at least 12 months), a green card and full insurance coverage.

Driving conditions: Drive on the right and pass on the left. Always yield right of way (unless otherwise indicated) to all vehicles coming from the right. Seat-belts, while not compulsory, are recommended.

Considering the mountainous terrain, the main roads of Madeira are better than might be expected. Never be complacent though: a nicely-banked, smooth, wide roadway usually evolves into a narrow, twisting washboard just when you least need a complication. Brakes and horns are in almost constant use on the island roads, with good reason. Perils are many: pedestrians, often undisciplined in safety rules; dogs that dislike cars; overloaded old lorries and buses. And you may run into sudden mist, rockslides in the mountains and pot-holes everywhere.

Speed limits: In towns, 60 kilometres per hour, otherwise 90 kph unless marked. In practice, however, the steep hills and hairpin bends inhibit most efforts at speeding; average cross-country speeds fall well below 60 kilometres per hour.

Traffic police: The police generally don't patrol the highways, but they do arrive at the scene of an accident. In Funchal, one or more traffic policemen keep cars moving during the rush hour.

Fuel and oil: Except for Funchal and the bigger towns, filling stations are scarce. The difficult mountain driving gulps more fuel than you expect, so it's wise to fill up your tank whenever you have a chance and to keep a jerry-can reserve of petrol just in case.

Fluid measures

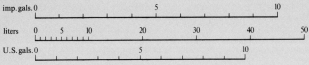

imp. gals. 0 — 5 — 10

liters 0 5 10 20 30 40 50

U.S. gals. 0 — 5 — 10

Distance

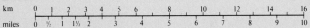

km 0 1 2 3 4 5 6 8 10 12 14 16

miles 0 ½ 1 1½ 2 3 4 5 6 7 8 9 10

Breakdowns: Well-equipped garages operate in Funchal and some other towns. In less populous areas local mechanics are often able to help or passing drivers may pitch in.

Road signs: The standard international picture-signs are used on Madeira. But you'll encounter some written notices as well. Among the more frequently seen:

Alto	Halt
Bermas baixas	Keep off the verge (Soft shoulder)
Cruzamento	Crossroads
Curva perigosa	Dangerous bend (curve)
Descida íngreme	Steep hill
Desvio	Diversion (detour)
Encruzilhada	Crossroads
Estacionamento permitido	Parking allowed
Estacionamento proíbido	No parking
Guiar com cuidado	Drive with care
Obras	Road works (men working)
Paragem de autocarro	Bus stop
Pare	Stop
Passagem proíbida	No entry
Pedestres, peões	Pedestrians
Perigo	Danger
Posto de socorros	First-aid post
Proíbida a entrada	No entry
Saída de camiões	Lorry (truck) exit
Seguir pela direita/esquerda	Keep right/left
Sem saída	No through road
Sentido proíbido	No entry

111

D

Sentido único	One-way street
Silêncio	Silence zone
Stop	Stop
Trabalhos	Road works (men working)
Trânsito proíbido	No through traffic
Veículos pesados	Alternative route for heavy vehicles
Velocidade máxima	Maximum speed

Parking: There are some restrictions in the centre of Funchal, so you may have to prowl a few streets to find a place. Several car parks have opened in Funchal. Illegal parking could cost from 5,000 escudos in fines.

Can I park here?	**Posso estacionar aqui?**
Are we on the right road for...?	**É esta a estrada para...?**
Fill the tank, please...	**Encha o depósito de..., por favor.**
normal/super	**normal/super**
Would you please change this tire?	**Pode mudar o pneu, por favor?**
Check the oil/tires/battery, please.	**Verifique o ólio/os pneus/ a bateria, se faz favor.**
I've had a breakdown.	**O meu carro está avariado.**
There's been an accident.	**Houve um acidente.**

DRUGS. On Madeira as in continental Portugal, the authorities take stern action against drug smugglers and traders.

E **ELECTRIC CURRENT** *(corrente eléctrica).* Everywhere on Madeira the standard is 220-volt, 50- (or occasionally 60-) cycle A.C. Transformers and plug adaptors are required for American appliances.

If your appliance should break down, ask your hotel receptionist to recommend an *electricista* or local handyman.

I need..., please.	**Preciso de..., por favor.**
an adaptor/a battery	**um adaptor/uma bateria.**

EMERGENCIES *(urgência).* Your hotel receptionist or travel-agency courier will usually have a ready solution to any problem. If they're not available or the case is too urgent to wait, here are some key telephone numbers:

Police, ambulance	115	
Fire	2 21 22	(Funchal)
	96 21 33	(Machico)
	5 21 63	(Santa Cruz)

ENTRY and CUSTOMS FORMALITIES *(alfândega).* American, British, Canadian and Irish citizens need only a valid passport—no visa—to visit Madeira or Portugal, and even this requirement is waived for the British who may enter on the simplified Visitor's Passport. Though residents of Europe and North America aren't subject to any health requirements, visitors from further afield should check with a travel agent before departure in case any inoculation certificates are called for.

Import allowances:

Into:	Cigarettes		Cigars		Tobacco	Spirits	Wine
Portugal 1)	300	or	75	or	400 g.	1½ l. and 5 l.	
2)	200	or	50	or	250 g.	1 l. and 2 l.	
Australia	200	or	250 g. or		250 g.	1 l. or 1 l.	
Canada	200	and	50	and	900 g.	1.1 l. or 1.1 l.	
Eire	200	or	50	or	250 g.	1 l. and 2 l.	
N. Zealand	200	or	50	or	250 g.	1.1 l. and 4.5 l.	
S. Africa	400	and	50	and	250 g.	1 l. and 2 l.	
U.K.	200	or	50	or	250 g.	1 l. and 2 l.	
U.S.A.	200	and	100	and	3)	1 l. or 1 l.	

1) From EEC countries.
2) From other countries.
3) A reasonable quantity.

E **Currency restrictions:** Visitors from abroad can bring any amount of local or foreign currency into Portugal, but sums exceeding the equivalent of 1,000,000 escudos in foreign currency must be declared on arrival. When leaving the country, you may take out foreign currency up to the amount imported and declared. No more than 100,000 escudos in local money may be exported per person per trip.

I've nothing to declare.	**Não tenho nada a declarar.**
It's for my personal use.	**É para uso pessoal.**

G **GUIDES*.** Arrangements can be made through a travel agent. All guides must belong to the professional association of guides and meet their standards. A guide or interpreter can be hired directly through their association in Funchal at

Rua Dr. Brito da Câmara, 4, apt. 103, tel. 2 65 24.

For guided tours you should check with a travel agent for information on both half- or full-day tours.

We'd like an English-speaking guide/an English interpreter.	**Queremos um guia que fale inglês/um intérprete de inglês.**

H **HAIRDRESSERS*.** Men's barbers are called *barbeiros*, women's and unisex salons, *cabeleireiros.* For tipping suggestions, see Tipping.

The following vocabulary will help:

I'd like a shampoo and set.	**Queria um champô e mise.**
I want a ...	**Quero ...**
haircut	**um corte**
razor cut	**um corte à navalha**
blow-dry (brushing)	**um brushing**
permanent wave	**uma permanente**
colour chart	**um mostruário de cores**
colour rinse	**uma rinsage**
manicure	**uma manicura**
Don't cut it too short.	**Não corte muito curto.**
A little more off (here).	**Corte mais um pouco (aqui).**

HITCH-HIKING *(boleia)*. The legality of hitch-hiking in Portugal is questionable but the practice is increasingly common. However, on Madeira, it's not frequently seen—or done.

Can you give us a lift to …?   **Pode levar-nos a …?**

HOTELS and ACCOMMODATION*. Hotels throughout Portugal are officially inspected and classified from one star up to five (luxury class). The simpler sorts of hostelries are called *albergarias, pensões* and *estalagens.* The government runs a renowned network of *pousadas* (inns), cheap and quaint and beautifully located; Madeira has two, one at Pico Ariero and the other at Vinhaticos.

Madeira can claim more than its share of top-class hotels offering almost every imaginable luxury from swimming pools and saunas to nightclubs and dog kennels, but on the other end of the scale you can have a double room with bath in a *pensão* for a fraction of the cost!

When you arrive at your hotel, inn or other, you'll receive a form which sets out the conditions, prices and room number. Continental breakfast is included in the cost of a room.

I'd like a single/double room.   **Queria um quarto simples/duplo.**

with bath/shower   **com banho/chuveiro**

What's the rate per night?   **Qual é o preço por noite?**

LANGUAGE. The language of Madeira is Portuguese, a derivative of Latin which at first hearing may sound slightly Slavic or like Spanish spoken with a Chinese intonation, or perhaps like a tape played backwards. Visitors from continental Portugal say the islanders speak slowly but enunciate poorly. They also use some purely local vocabulary, occasionally producing puzzlement among "foreigners" from the mainland. English is widely understood.

The Berlitz phrase book PORTUGUESE FOR TRAVELLERS covers most situations you're likely to encounter during a visit to Madeira. Also useful is the Portuguese-English/English-Portuguese pocket dictionary, containing a special menu-reader supplement.

A few words to get you going:

Good morning/Good evening	**Bom dia/Boa noite**
Please	**Por favor**
Thank you	**Obrigado/Obrigada (fem.)**
Good-bye	**Adeus**
Yes/No	**Sim/Não**

L **LAUNDRY and DRY-CLEANING.** Hotels handle your laundry and dry-cleaning problems swiftly and efficiently. Since there is only one coin-operated launderette, your alternatives are limited.

When will it be ready?	**Quando estará pronto?**
I must have this for tomorrow morning.	**Preciso disto para amanhã de manhã.**

LOST PROPERTY. Inquire first at your hotel desk or the tourist office. Then report the loss to the local police station.

Lost children. If a child gets lost on a beach, inquire at the nearest beach bar or restaurant. In towns, a lost child would be delivered to the police station which is where you should go if you lose a child—or find one.

I've lost my ...	**Perdi ...**
wallet/bag/passport	**a minha carteira/o meu saco/ o meu passaporte**

M **MAPS.** The tourist office in Funchal issues a useful road map of Madeira with a street plan of the capital on the reverse side. Certain travellers may be interested in much more detailed maps published by the Instituto Geográfico e Cadastral obtainable at local bookshops. The maps in this guide were prepared by Falk-Verlag, Hamburg.

a street plan of Funchal	**uma planta da cidade de Funchal**
a road map of this island	**um mapa das estradas desta ilha**

MEDICAL CARE. See also EMERGENCIES. Medical insurance to cover the risk of illness or accident while abroad is a worthwhile investment. Your travel agent or regular insurance company will have policies available.

There is a Health Services Information Centre for tourists at Rua das Pretas, 1, Funchal, as well as modern health centres around the island and on Porto Santo.

Farmácias (pharmacies) are open during normal business hours. In addition, one pharmacy in every town is always on duty around the clock. Its address is announced on the door of every other *farmácia*.

Where's the nearest (all-night) pharmacy?	**Onde fica a farmácia (de serviço) mais próxima?**
I need a doctor/dentist.	**Preciso de um médico/dentista.**
an ambulance	**uma ambulância**
hospital	**hospital**
sunburn	**queimadura de sol**
sunstroke	**uma insolação**
a fever	**febre**
an upset stomach	**dôr de estômago**
insect bite	**uma picadela de insecto**

MEETING PEOPLE. The Portuguese are reserved, so you may have to take the first step if you want to make friends. They'll react very warmly to your initiative. As everywhere, young people are more spontaneous and outgoing. People are less reserved at beaches and cafés than most other places.

Don't let it bother you if people, especially villagers, seem to be staring at you; it's only unaffected curiosity. On the other hand, it's somtimes difficult to catch the eye of a waiter when you need him. The Portuguese do not use an equivalent Portuguese word for "Waiter", but say *Faz favor* (Please!).

How do you do?	**Muito prazer.**
How are you?	**Como está?**
Very well, thank you.	**Muito bem, obrigado/obrigada** (fem.).

MONEY MATTERS

Currency. Don't be appalled when you see price tags quoting many digits punctuated by the $ sign. Here it means *escudo* (abbreviated *esc.*), not dollar; the sign normally replaces the decimal point (thus 5.000 $00 means 5,000 escudos). The escudo is divided into 100 *centavos*.

Coins: 1, 2½, 5, 10, 20, 50, 100, 200 esc.

Banknotes: 100, 500, 1,000 (equalling one *conto*), 5,000, 10,000 esc.

For currency restrictions, see ENTRY AND CUSTOMS FORMALITIES.

M **Banking hours** are from 8.30 a.m. to 2.45 p.m. (open at lunchtime), Monday to Friday. Currency-exchange offices are open longer. Your hotel will also change money, but at a less favourable rate.

Traveller's cheques are easily cashed but be sure to take your passport with you for identification. Eurocheques are also accepted.

Credit cards of the well-known international companies are accepted in major hotels, restaurants and tourist-orientated enterprises as well as in car hire agencies.

Prices. Compared with North European or American prices, things aren't notably expensive in Portugal—with two major exceptions, cars and the fuel to run them. Of course, everything is less in non-tourist establishments. Certain rates are listed on page 104 to give you an idea of what things cost.

Haggling is not done; prices are as marked.

Where's the nearest bank/ currency exchange office?	**Onde fica o banco mais próximo/ a casa de câmbio mais próxima?**
I want to change some pounds/dollars.	**Queria trocar libras/dólares.**
Can I cash a traveller's cheque?	**Posso trocar um cheque de viagem?**
Can I pay with this credit card?	**Posso pagar com este cartão de crédito?**
How much is that?	**Quanto custa isto?**

N **NEWSPAPERS and MAGAZINES** (*jornal; revista*). Europe's principal newspapers, including most British dailies and the *International Herald Tribune*, published in Paris, are regularly available the day after publication at many newsagents and hotels of Madeira. Popular foreign magazines are also sold at the same shops or stands. To check on cinema programmes and other activities on the island, see one of the local Portuguese-language dailies, *Jornal da Madeira* or *Diário de Notícias*. The monthly English *Madeira Island Bulletin* has local news and features of interest to tourists.

Hotels, news-stands and shops catering to tourists sell popular paperback books in English and some other languages.

Have you any English-language newspapers/magazines?	**Tem jornais/revistas em inglês?**

PHOTOGRAPHY. Well-known brands of film in all sizes are sold at photo shops, news-stands and many other outlets. One hour and same-day development service is to be found in the capital.

P

I'd like a film for this camera.	**Quero um rolo para esta máquina.**
a black-and-white film	**um rolo a preto e branco**
a colour film	**um rolo a cores**
a colour-slide film	**um rolo de diapositivos**
35-mm film	**um rolo de trinta e cinco milimetros**
super-8	**super oito**
How long will it take to develop this film?	**Quanto tempo leva a revelar este filme?**
May I take a picture?	**Posso tirar uma fotografia?**

POLICE *(polícia).* The national police, wearing grey uniforms, maintain public order and oversee the traffic. Rural police wear brown uniforms. In Funchal, you may see a policeman with a red armband marked *Turismo.* He can communicate in foreign languages and is expressly assigned to assist tourists.

Where's the nearest police station?	**Onde fica o posto de polícia mais próximo?**

PUBLIC HOLIDAYS *(feriado)*

Jan. 1	*Ano Novo*	New Year's Day
April 25	*Dia de Portugal*	National Day
May 1	*Dia do Trabalho*	Labour Day
June 10	*Dia de Camões*	Camoens' Day
Aug. 15	*Assunção*	Assumption
Oct. 5	*Dia da República*	Republic Day
Nov. 1	*Todos-os-Santos*	All Saints' Day
Dec. 1	*Restauração*	Restoration Day (of Independence)
Dec. 8	*Imaculada Conceição*	Immaculate Conception
Dec. 25	*Natal*	Christmas Day

119

P | Movable dates: | *Sexta-feira Santa* | Good Friday |
| | *Corpo de Deus* | Corpus Christi |

These are only the *national* holidays of Portugal. Many special holidays affect different branches of the economy of regions of the country. Madeira, for instance, has three local holidays—July 1 (in honour of the Discovery of Madeira), August 21 (municipal holiday) and December 26 (Boxing Day).

Are you open tomorrow? **Estão abertos amanhã?**

R **RADIO and TV** *(rádio; televisão)*. Madeira picks up by satellite many live programmes from the continent. Reception is excellent.

Madeira has three local radio stations. They broadcast in Portuguese, but one of the stations sets aside time for a foreign-language programme called "Madeira Tourist Radio".

Shortwave programmes of the Voice of America, BBC and other European stations can be picked up at certain times of day. Most broadcasts audible on Madeira are newscasts in English and French beamed to listeners in Africa.

RELIGIOUS SERVICES *(serviço religioso)*. The religion of Portugal (and Madeira) is Roman Catholic. Mass is said regularly in almost all of the island's churches, modern or historic. Every Sunday in winter, a Catholic service in English is held in Funchal's Igreja da Penha.

Anglican Sunday services are conducted in the English Church, Rua de Quebra Costas, Funchal, and there is also a Baptist Church, in Rua Cidade de Honolulu.

The Scottish Church, at the corner of Rua do Conselheiro and Rua Ivens, Funchal, has services on the first Sunday of each month.

The tourist office has service hours.

What time is mass/the service? **A que horas é a missa/o culto?**
Is it in English? **É em inglês?**

S **SHOPPING HOURS.** Most shops and offices are open from 9 a.m. to 1 p.m. and 3 to 7 p.m., Monday to Friday, and from 9 a.m. to 1 p.m. on Saturdays (shopping centres 9.30 a.m. to 10 p.m.). The **120** siesta is not observed here, but two hours for lunch is the norm.

TIME DIFFERENCES. Madeira (like mainland Portugal) is on Greenwich Mean Time. In summer clocks are put forward one hour.

Los Angeles	Chicago	New York	**Madeira**	London
4 a.m.	6 a.m.	7 a.m.	**noon**	noon

What time is it, please?   **Que horas são, por favor?**

TIPPING. Hotel and restaurant bills are generally all-inclusive, though waiters are given an additional tip if service has been good. It is also in order to hand the bellboys, doormen, filling-station attendants, etc., gratuities for their services. The chart below gives some suggestions as to what to give.

Hotel porter, per bag	50–100 esc.
Hotel maid, per week	500–1,000 esc.
Lavatory attendant	25 esc.
Waiter	10%
Taxi driver	10%
Hairdresser/Barber	10%
Tour guide	10%

TOILETS (*lavabos/toiletes*). Public conveniences are strategically located in several towns of Madeira. If there's an attendant on duty, a small tip would be appropriate. "Ladies" in *Senhoras* and "Gentlemen", *Homens*.

Where are the toilets?   **Onde ficam os toiletes?**

TOURIST INFORMATION OFFICES. The Portuguese government maintains tourist offices in more than a dozen foreign countries.

T Here are some addresses:

Canada: Suite 704, Canada Square, 2200 Yonge Street, Toronto, Ont. M4S 2C6; tel. (416) 485-9004.

1801 McGill College Avenue, Montreal. Que. H3A 2N4; tel. (514) 282-1264.

U.S.A.: 548 Fifth Avenue, New York, NY 10036; tel. (212) 354-4403.

Suite 3001, 969 Michigan Avenue, Chicago, IL 60611; tel. (312) 266-9898.

Suite 616, 3640 Wilshire Boulevard, Los Angeles, CA 90010; tel. (213) 580-6459.

Great Britain: New Bond Street House, 1–5, New Bond Street, London W1Y ODB; tel. (071) 493-3873.

On Madeira itself, there's a helpful government tourist office at Avenida Arriaga 18, Funchal (tel.: 2 56 58)

where multilingual personnel will be able to answer your questions, offer advice and provide you with maps and brochures.

Where's the tourist office? **Onde fica o oficio do turismo?**

TRANSPORT

Buses* *(autocarro).* Bus services take care of transport needs both within Funchal and to its environs, as well as running schedules to outlying districts. It is possible to see most of the island without much difficulty using buses. Timetables with maps and explanations of the route numbering system are available at the tourist office in Funchal.

Vehicles range from streamlined expresses to antique models. On most buses you pay the driver on entry (or buy a block of tickets from the offices on Avenida do Mar). Hold on to your ticket in case an inspector comes aboard to double-check. Bus stops are identified by a sign reading *Paragem.*

Taxis* *(taxi).* Taxis are painted yellow and blue. The letter "A"—for taxis in country areas—is prominently marked on the front doors. There are taxi ranks in many areas of Funchal and in most villages. If there is only one passenger, it's customary for him to sit beside the driver. Taxis are metered. You can hire a taxi for sightseeing. For some prices see page 104.

Trains. You've missed the last one. In 1943, because of wartime problems, the funicular railway from Funchal to Monte and Terreiro da Luta, more than 50 years old, was closed. Buses now cover the route more efficiently and toboggans more dramatically.

I want a ticket to …	**Queria um bilhete para …**
single (one-way)	**ida**
return (round-trip)	**ida e volta**
Will you tell me when to get off?	**Pode dizer-me quando devo descer?**
Where can I get a taxi?	**Onde posso encontrar um táxi?**

WATER *(água)*. The tap water of Madeira—fresh as a mountain brook—is not only potable but quite tasty. It lacks minerals, though, so Madeirans and long-time visitors often ask for bottled water from Porto Santo Island for a healthy change.

a bottle of mineral water	**uma garrafa de água mineral**
carbonated	**com gás**
non-carbonated	**sem gás**

YOUTH HOSTELS. No such facilities on Madeira, but young travellers shouldn't be discouraged; very economical accommodation may be found in small *pensões* (boarding houses).

DAYS OF THE WEEK

Sunday	**domingo**	Thursday	**quinta-feira**
Monday	**segunda-feira**	Friday	**sexta-feira**
Tuesday	**terça-feira**	Saturday	**sábado**
Wednesday	**quarta-feira**		

MONTHS

January	**Janeiro**	July	**Julho**
February	**Fevereiro**	August	**Agosto**
March	**Março**	September	**Setembro**
April	**Abril**	October	**Outubro**
May	**Maio**	November	**Novembro**
June	**Junho**	December	**Dezembro**

NUMBERS

0	**zero**	19	**dezanove**
1	**um**	20	**vinte**
2	**dois**	21	**vinte e um**
3	**três**	22	**vinte e dois**
4	**quatro**	23	**vinte e três**
5	**cinco**	30	**trinta**
6	**seis**	40	**quarenta**
7	**sete**	50	**cinquenta**
8	**oito**	60	**sessenta**
9	**nove**	70	**setenta**
10	**dez**	71	**setenta e um**
11	**onze**	80	**oitenta**
12	**doze**	90	**noventa**
13	**treze**	100	**cem**
14	**catorze**	101	**cento e um**
15	**quinze**	200	**duzentos**
16	**dezasseis**	300	**trezentos**
17	**dezassete**	500	**quinhentos**
18	**dezoito**	1000	**mil**

SOME USEFUL EXPRESSIONS

yes/no	**sim/não**
please/thank you	**faz favor/obrigado (obrigada)**
excuse me/you're welcome	**perdão/de nada**
where/when/how	**onde/quando/como**
how long/how far	**quanto tempo/a que distância**
yesterday/today/tomorrow	**ontem/hoje/amanhã**
day/week/month/year	**dia/semana/mês/ano**
left/right	**esquerdo/direito**
good/bad	**bom/mau**
big/small	**grande/pequeno**
cheap/expensive	**barato/caro**
hot/cold	**quente/frio**
old/new	**velho/novo**
open/closed	**aberto/fechado**
up/down	**em cima/em baixo**
here/there	**aqui/ali**
free (vacant)/occupied	**livre/ocupado**
early/late	**cedo/tarde**
easy/difficult	**fácil/difícil**
I don't speak Portuguese.	**Não falo português.**
Does anyone here speak English?	**Alguém fala inglês?**
What does this mean?	**Que quer dizer isto?**
I don't understand.	**Não compreendo.**
Please write it down.	**Escreva-mo, por favor.**
Is there an admission charge?	**Paga-se entrada?**
Waiter!/Waitress!	**Faz favor!**
I'd like …	**Queria …/Quero …**
How much is that?	**Quanto custa isto?**
Have you something less expensive?	**Tem qualquer coisa de mais barato?**
Just a minute.	**Um momento.**
What time is it?	**Que horas são?**
Help me, please.	**Ajude-me, por favor.**
Get a doctor, quickly.	**Chame um médico, depressa.**

Index

An asterisk (*) next to a page number indicates a map reference.